The Blue Max Airmen
German Airmen Awarded the Pour le Mérite
Volume 2
Buddecke, Wintgens, Mulzer

Lance J. Bronnenkant, PhD.

The Blue Max Airmen
German Airmen Awarded the Pour le Mérite
Volume 2
Buddecke, Wintgens, Mulzer
Lance J. Bronnenkant, PhD.

I would like to thank and acknowledge the *Kommunalarchiv* Minden (particularly Vinzenz Lübben) and the following colleagues who so generously assisted in the creation of this work: Bruno Couplez, Reinhard Kastner, Terry Phillips, Josef Scott, Manfred Thiemeyer, Alfonso Guerrina Valeta and Tobias Weber.
– Lance J. Bronnenkant

Interested in WWI aviation? Join The League of WWI Aviation Historians (**www.overthefront.com**) and Cross & Cockade International (**www.crossandcockade.com**)

Text © 2012 Lance J. Bronnenkant, PhD.
Design and layout: Jack Herris
Cover design: Aaron Weaver
Aircraft Colors and Markings: Greg VanWyngarden
Color Profiles: Jim Miller
Digital photo editing: Aaron Weaver & Jack Herris
Printed in USA by Walsworth Publishing Company

www.aeronautbooks.com

Publisher's Cataloging-in-Publication data

Bronnenkant, Lance J.
   The Blue Max Airmen: German Aviators Awarded the Pour le Mérite: Volume 2 / by Lance J. Bronnenkant.
      p. cm.
   ISBN 978-1-935881-06-3
1. Buddecke, Hans-Joachim, 1891–1916. 2. Wintgens, Kurt, 1890–1916. 3. Mulzer, Max Ritter von 4. World War, 1914–1918 --Aerial operations, German. 5. Fighter pilots --Germany. 6. Aeronautics, Military --Germany -- History. II. Title.

ND237 .S6322 2011
759.13 --dc22   2011904920

Table of Contents

Hans-Joachim Buddecke

Oberleutnant Buddecke,
zurzeit in türkiſchen Dienſten, erhielt den Orden Pour le Mérite.

This announcement of Hans-Joachim Buddecke's receipt of the *Orden Pour le Mérite* was presented in the 6 May 1916 edition of *Die Woche* (19, p.657). The photograph, taken soon after Buddecke's award ceremony, was later reproduced by Willi Sanke as number 371 in his famous postcard series featuring German aviators.

Buddecke – The Man

Youth and Early Career

Not much is known today about Hans-Joachim Buddecke's family and early life. What we do know is that his father was Albert Buddecke (1858–1931), a career army officer who published several military treatises and rose to the rank of *Oberst* (colonel) before his death in Jena.[1] He married Anna Herber (1864–1950) and together they had three sons. The eldest was Werner (1887–1967), who was badly wounded in France during the early part of the war but survived to serve in the Army Command's central library. Their second son was Hartmut (1888–

1945), who commanded *Grosstorpedoboot* (torpedo boat destroyer) *V27* during the Battle of Jutland/ Skaggerak as an *Oblt.z.See* and later patented a fire extinguisher in several countries.[2] Then came their brother, Adolf August Hans-Joachim Buddecke, who was born in Berlin on 22 August 1890. He went to school in Potsdam, Strasbourg and Charlottenburg before entering the Cadet Corps in the spring of 1904 and was admitted to the Selekta, a special cadet course considered to be preparation for the War Academy and eventual service with the general staff. He passed his final examination in 1910 and was posted as a *Leutnant* to his father's former unit, *Leibgarde-Infanterie-Regiment* (1. *Grossherzoglich*

Right: Hans-Joachim Buddecke, commanding officer of *Jasta* 4, and his older brother, Hartmut, pose together at the unit's quarters near Roupy in the first half of October 1916.

Below: The Buddecke brothers are alone in the first picture while the second shows them in company with various *Jasta* 4 members (left to right): *Lt.* Eberhardt Fügner, *Lt.* Leo Strauch, *Lt.* Trentepohl, *Oblt.* Ernst von Althaus, *Oblt.z.See* Hartmut Buddecke, *Lt.* Hans Malchow, *Oblt.* Hans-Joachim Buddecke, *Lt.* Wilhelm Frankl, *Lt.* Joachim von Ziegesar, unknown naval officer, two unknowns, *Lt.* Fritz Otto Bernert, *Lt.* Karl Stehle, *Vzfw.* Josef Veltjens.

Hessisches) Nr. 115. Three years later his little cousin, while visiting him in Berlin, suggested: "Oh, Hans, you must come see us in America; you would have a very fine time." It proved to be an irresistable temptation: "I was in uniform – I was a *Leutnant* in a Guard Regiment – and wore it as proudly as anyone could; but here an opportunity was offered to me to go out into the world and see a bit of it."[3] After resigning from full time military service to become

a reservist, Buddecke traveled to Indianapolis where his uncle lived. At first, just as his cousin had promised, "the first few days were very beautiful and merry... but after all, I had not come over for that. So I went to my uncle to discuss the matter. All of a sudden, when our talk turned to business, he was no longer the relative who had welcomed me with open arms but a sober American businessman who was only concerned with the numbers. 'So, what can you

Facing Page & Above: Many of those assigned to *Ettapen-Flugzeug-Park* 2 near Bellenglise stayed at the nearby Chateau Grand-Priel. These two photos were taken while Buddecke was there (note the absence of a Pilot's Badge or any other decorations). He is standing third from the left on the balcony in the first picture and at far left in the front row of the second, which appears to have been taken close to Christmas. Also in the second, seated on the balcony third from the right, is then *Lt.* Rudolf Berthold who first met and became good friends with Buddecke at *Ettapen-Flugzeug-Park* 2.

do?' What could I do? My cadet education and my training as a *Leutnant* had not particularly burdened me with too much practical knowledge. Ordering someone to tie up a dress tie, if necessary, that I could do, but otherwise... so I stayed silent. 'You do have some technical knowledge, right? Particularly some understanding of automobiles?' Hold on, now there was a lifesaver. Some understanding of automobiles? I was really interested in them. Even though up to now cars had captured my attention only as a means of locomotion, still – there was also a real technical interest. So I said, 'Yes.'" Buddecke's uncle, who owned several factories, placed him in one that made automobile parts – but it was not a cushy position. "Now I had achieved what I had been striving for: I was standing on my own two feet. But where and how? At a vice, ten hours a

day, sometimes even on Sundays. My hands were rough and callused... everything was different, but I gritted my teeth and carried on."[4] Buddecke worked at the job for months, getting to know "the poor people, the dear people who spent their lives there." He was proud that he got to know them "not as a disguised gentleman, but as a real journeyman."[5] But he knew he could make more of himself. He studied books on mathematics, engineering and design for nine months until he finally resolved to become a builder of airplanes. When the automobile parts factory temporarily suspended work, Buddecke traveled around the country and met two men named Orr and Linn in Chicago. They had bought a Nieuport monoplane in Europe and shipped it to Chicago where they hoped to replicate it and thereby establish an airplane manufacturing business. Their duplicate cost them seven times more to build than the original, however, so they abandoned their idea and put both Nieuports up for sale. Buddecke approached his uncle with his own business plan and was given the means to buy one (the duplicate), which he did in the spring of 1914. Now that he had his own airplane, he only had to figure out how to fly it! But first, he upgraded the powerplant from a 35 hp engine to a 50 hp Gnome. He also purchased a second set of wings in case of accident. Then he completely familiarized himself with his purchase until the ground had sufficiently dried up to allow a test run at the Chicago airfield where the plane was hangared. The day of reckoning was near. Around five o-clock the next morning, hoping that no one would be there "to admire maneuvers beneath human dignity," his assistant started the engine and Buddecke rolled around the field at quarter-power[6]. Whenever he wanted to go straight ahead under more power though, the plane veered to the left and dug its wingtip into the ground. Disconcerted, Buddecke rolled it back into its hangar for the night and contemplated what to do next. He came to a conclusion and the next morning tried it out: "Full power. Just as my animal wanted to go to the left, I firmly threw the rudder to the right; and see there, it returned and went straight ahead with the tail rising. I became anxious and immediately cut the engine to put an end to the the maneuver. But while still rolling, I innocently and naively pulled the steering mechanism back to my stomach and suddenly found myself up in the air. But before I could do anything about it myself, the plane had already touched down hard on the earth and come to a standstill. I... got out, spent fifteen minutes in hard thought and said to myself: 'at the start much rudder, full power, and the beast will take care of the rest if you only just pay attention and keep calm.'"[7] And with that, Buddecke took off around the Chicago field on his first successful flight.

Buddecke flew the plane constantly during the following weeks and also set his plan for establishing his own manufacturing facility in motion. "Letters flew in all directions and materials were obtained... then the war came and brought new experiences."[8]

Buddecke had to make his way back to Germany from the United States. He went to New York City and used an assumed name, Morice Adolph, to book passage on the Greek steamship *Athene*. At the ticket office, "the woman laughed when I haltingly signed the unusual name; she did not seem to completely believe me."[9] English and French warships passed close alongside the steamer during the ocean crossing but did not stop to board her. After the ship docked at Palermo, Buddecke made his way to Rome and Verona and then caught a train to Munich where he set foot on German soil after an almost two-year absence.

Airman

Because of his flying interest and experience, Buddecke volunteered to join the *Fliegertruppe* (Air Service) at the beginning of the war. He was immediately assigned to a *Flieger-Ersatz-Abteilung* at Darmstadt on 2 September, transferred to *Flieger-Ersatz-Abteilung* 3 near Reims on 27 September, moved again to *Ettapen-Flugzeug-Park* 2 near Bellenglisse on 20 October, and then on to *Feldflieger-Abteilung* 27 on 12 January 1915. It was there that he passed the formal flight examinations that earned him his Pilot's Badge. Photographic evidence tells us that he also received at least two decorations while serving with *FFA* 27. The ribbon for his Iron Cross, 2nd Class is clearly evident in the buttonhole of his tunic in an *FFA* 27 group picture (see below). Underneath it is a ribbon that could only have been for Bavaria's Military Merit Order, 4th Class with Swords, because we know that all of his remaining decorations that carried ribbons were awarded to him after his tenure with *FFA* 27.

The first two-seaters designed to carry a machine gun arrived at the Front in the early summer of 1915 and it was around then that *FFA* 27 received one. It was kept ready for action at all times and Buddecke was assigned to its second shift crew. He soon discovered, however, that he did not like the airplane much: "...the apparatus was of such inferior construction... that it could not do a steep turning curve and needed minutes for a 90 degree turn. When my *Abteilung* commander asked what I thought about it, I did not hide my opinion from him." Buddecke was also aware of the new Fokker *Eindecker* fighter that had appeared at the Front and said that it was the ideal way to fight in the air. "My *Abteilung* leader had a different opinion, so I asked for a transfer. This certainly does not mean that I do not admire him to this very day – and not just because he carries the *Pour le Mérite*."[10] Though Buddecke never identified the man (or *FFA* 27) in his autobiography, *El Schahin (Der Jagdfalke)*, we know it was Alfred Keller who earned the *Pour le Mérite* on 4 December 1917 when he was the CO of *Kampfgeschwader* 1.

Hptm. Karl Seber, *FFA* 23's CO, requested that Buddecke join his unit at the behest of one of his men, Rudolf Berthold, who had befriended Buddecke during the fighting around Reims in September 1914. Upon his arrival on 10 June 1915, Buddecke was given a new machine to fly that he found quite satisfactory and used on several reconnaissance

Above: This is a group photo of *FFA* 27 when Buddecke served with the unit. In the front row, from left to right: Buddecke, von Mudra, *Hptm*. Alfred Keller (CO), Baur-Betaz, Müller. Behind them (left to right): Volck, (possibly *Oblt*. Günther) Viehweger, *Rittm*. Anton von Brederlow (wounded 9 May 1917 as CO of *Jasta* 17), Demmel, *Hptm*. Kurt Schmikali (wounded 22 October 1916 with *KEK* Metz, died next day), *Oblt*. Kurt Drobnig (killed 7 June 1916 with *FAA* 221), von Sillich, *Lt*. Hans Reitter (killed 8 December 1915), *Dr*. Fantel. The dogs were named Kiwi (held by Demmel) and Joffre (forefront). (photo courtesy of Tobias Weber)

missions. During one of them, he barely escaped with his life after French pre-war aviator Jules Védrines attacked him and set the flares that Buddecke carried on board ablaze. Buddecke also got his wish when he was given a chance to fly the unit's Fokker *Eindecker*, "...which hardly anyone else wanted to have."[11] After that, it took just three weeks until he was able to achieve his first victory in it.

Fighter Pilot

Buddecke gave the following account of his first victory, which occurred on 19 September 1915 when he downed BE.2c 2008, manned by 2Lt. W.H. Nixon (pilot) and Capt. J.N.S. Stott (observer) of RFC No.8 Squadron: "It was at the end of September 1915, around noon on Sunday when I ascended

in my *Eindecker* from Chateau Vaux (where the small fighting unit belonging to Roupy's main squadron had set up camp) toward where English reconnaissance planes were always making trouble over Bapaume-le Chateau-St. Quentin-Péronne. I was above St. Quentin about two kilometers to the south when a yellow-brown something appeared and grew sharper in the bluish high-altitude haze. What was it? My eyes locked on it, did not let it go, while one hand pulled the lever to make the machine gun ready to fire. Our machines slowly closed on one another until his brown wings grew plainly visible. Cockades! They were like a red flag. Cockades – and with them only one sentiment: either you or me. Before long I was above him; my excitement was at its peak. I had no clear plan, but only made each movement and turn by pure instinct. I nosed

Left: The remains of Buddecke's first victim, BE.2c 2008 of RFC No.8 Squadron. Buddecke stated that it had received 108 hits.

my machine straight down, fell on him, aimed and shot. Meanwhile, 2Lt. Nixon awoke from his dream. He was probably thinking of the pretty girl whose picture he carried in his breast pocket. His observer, Capt. Stotts [SIC], also turned his attention from the lines that he had been busily studying on the ground below to the approaching danger up above... Between my dive and the forward motion of my opponent – which was a full-fuselaged biplane of the usual type – I reached his altitude about 200 meters behind him.[12] I looked through the rectangular sight, drew a bead on the silhouette and fired. Tack-tack...tack-tack...tack...tack...tack. It kept going. I carefully thought...range?...something was off... go a little bit to the left. The other side diligently responded: Tack-tack...tack...tack...tack...tack. Then the cook, who had just served a chicken meal, rushed into Roupy's dining hall with the big piece of news: A Fokker was shooting! Then they threw the knives and forks aside and rushed outside in order to watch and be witnesses. Who knows who was more excited – me or the people below? Those who saw a comrade in a duel or the French women on the village street who folded their hands in prayer for a victory for their side? In the meantime, destiny was being fulfilled above. Stott was a good shot. After a little shooting, however, one of my bullets hit his gun's mechanism and put it out of commission. He pulled his semiautomatic pistol from his holster and shot off nine rounds. Shots whistled around him incessantly. When he tried to reload, the gun was ripped from his hands; and now he was certain to be hit because his opponent was only ten meters away. He glanced at Nixon. He saw how his head fell forward as the entire airplane tilted and fell into

the depths. Then he summoned up all his strength, climbed out onto the wing of the plunging machine, swung himself into the pilot's seat onto his dying comrade's shoulders, pressed his heels down on the man's knees in order to operate the foot pedals and snatched the control column from his stiffening hands. I just sat between my wings and let my gun hammer him... I was surprised that there was no sign of any effect whatsoever over there; and I was even more surprised at how securely my steering could keep my opponent's entire machine on the bead of my gunsight as we turned. I was about ten meters from the tail of my enemy. Those are the most precious times. Every shot hits... And just at that moment, when I thought I had triumphed, Stott's god of luck in the form of a wind gust tore the leather end of my cartridge belt free from its container – the machine gun faltered. I veered off, turned and circled, and as quickly as possible retrieved the belt, which had entangled itself back in the elevator control link, until it was back in place. When I spotted my opponent again, he was lower than me. I went down. Quickly, I was behind him again. I did not shoot any more because I hoped he would go down peacefully. Then, however, I saw the following: a man, with a wind-inflated, light yellow leather jacket towering up from the pilot's compartment. I cannot explain it, but I suspected something was going on over there. I sensed there was something wrong and prepared myself. We slid down several meters, turning, until my opponent gave off vapor trails, climbed steeply and began to fly forward under full power. His final attempt to escape. I immediatey closed my left eye again. The engine growled mechanically and I shot – at the

Above: German soldiers gather the remains of Buddecke's second victim (BE.2c 2017 of RFC No.13 Squadron) for transport away from its crash site. The plane reportedly had 212 bullet holes in it. (photo courtesy of Alfonso Guerrina Valeta)

yellow, billowed leather jacket. After a while, the enemy lowered his nose and spiraled toward the ground. I followed turn by turn and saw how the enemy plane's shadow flitted over the fields and streets below and drew closer and closer to the earth. I was pretty pleased with my 'peacock butterfly.'[13] Glaring sunlight shone on the fields among the patches of forest east of Caulaincourt. The giant bird dove in there, burst in a thick cloud of dust and the four blue-white-red cockades lay lifeless on the ground. A line soldier plucked up his courage and, leading fifty others, approached the site while I flew back to my hangar near Vaux. Cars filled with men rolled out to the crash site. I got into one. Before we got to the place, we stopped. I got out and asked how things were. They said one was dead. I let the others drive on and went into the village where the prisoner should be. I have never viewed such a dead person, and have guarded against impressions that might

stay with one the rest of one's life – or were even sad. So I went there and spoke to Stott, who then told me exactly what had happened. Laughing, he showed me his clothes and yellow leather jacket. They were completely torn to pieces. 'You are some shot,' he said. The French hostess who was housing him served lunch to both of us. Like most Englishmen when they are by themselves, he was a good, open man who was not lacking in friendship – an experience I have often had. But when there is more than one, then everything is quite different. In front of one another, they do not have the honest courage to accept a German. When I later visited Stott in Saint-Quentin and told him that I had shot down another of his comrades, he just shook his head and made the somewhat understandable suggestion that in their interest I should immediately go on a four week leave."[14] It is interesting, and perhaps characteristic of Buddecke, that at times

Above & Facing Page: Buddecke downed his third victory, BE.2c 1725, on 11 November 1915. Lt. W.A. Harvey of RFC No.8 Squadron, minus his observer in order to compensate for the weight of the bombs he was carrying, was participating in a raid on a German airfield at Bellenglise when he was wounded and forced to touch down near Saint-Quentin (he later died of tuberculosis on 7 November 1917 while interned in Switzerland). The first image shows the essentially intact plane at its landing site. The second was snapped after it had been removed to a more secure location. (second photo courtesy of Alfonso Guerrina Valeta)

this account comes off as more of a tribute to his opponent than to himself. On 16 October 1915, in recognition of this victory, Saxony awarded him its Knight's Cross of the Military St. Henry Order.

One week later, on 23 October 1915, Buddecke had a slow start to the day: "When my orderly came into the room to wake me up, I had a rather 'heavy head.' He drew the curtains open. A wonderful, thick cloud cover hung down almost to the ground. Then my orderly picked up my military clothes, which were strewn about the room, and went out again. I rolled over onto my other side, to rest for just a moment. After what seemed like five minutes, my orderly returned and maintained that I had slept for three hours! So. I slowly remembered... the group of comrades... Mumm... observer Schüler... I was supposed to fly for the Duke of Brunswick... that's right, the duke and Prince August Wilhelm wanted to come here. Ach, and my head hummed so."[15] Much to Buddecke's dismay, the weather cleared and the afternoon's "big program" (as Buddecke called it) was still on. But just before the royal visitors arrived, enemy aircraft were reported in the vicinity and an alarm was raised. Buddecke, standing in his best uniform next to *FFA* 23's two *Eindeckers*, quickly donned his flight gear and took off in one of them. He caught up with BE.2c 2017 from RFC

No.13 Squadron somewhere between Roupy and Vaux-en-Vermandois and made four or five diving passes before he killed the plane's observer, 2Lt. W.G. Lawrence (brother of the famous T.E Lawrence, a.k.a. 'Lawrence of Arabia'), and seriously wounded its pilot, Capt. C.H. Marks, who in his dying minutes appears to have tried to bring the plane down in a slow descent. Buddecke cautiously trailed behind, withholding his fire; but then *Oblt.* Ernst von Althaus arrived on the scene in *FFA* 23's other Fokker and, unaware of the crew's plight, dove on the BE.2c and administered the *coup de grâce*. The plane crashed immediately in full view of an army of spectators, including Duke Ernst August and Prince August Wilhelm.[16] Buddecke landed back at Vaux and was treated to the cheers of hundreds of men.

Then Rudolf Berthold returned from a mission that he had conducted in one of *FFA* 23's two-seaters 120 kilometers behind enemy lines near Abbeville. The side of his observer's seat had been blown away by shrapnel from an antiaircraft shell that had passed between the man's legs, just missing him. They all had just removed their flight clothes when the Duke and Prince arrived at the field. The unit's Fokker fighters were lined up again and the "big program" commenced while Buddecke and Berthold stood in the background "with faces still flushed red from

excitement." The day was not over for Buddecke though. He and Althaus were told to take the *Eindeckers* off in tandem, which they did. Then they engaged in sideways maneuvers that were intended "to delight the spectators." During one of them, however, Althaus passed too close to Buddecke who had to pull up to avoid a collision. Althaus dove and tried to straighten out when his engine suddenly quit. His speed was too high during the resulting forced landing and his Fokker rolled up to a road embankment where its undercarriage collapsed, causing the plane to flip over on its back. Althaus emerged unscathed except for his pride. Then Buddecke landed so badly that he almost cracked up too. The spectators moved on to the biplane display where fortunately, a simulated bombing mission was carried off much more smoothly. Far from being embarrassed, Buddecke's account makes it clear that he found their performance to have been somewhat humorous. He noted that "the Royal Highnesses eventually came around to the opinion that our acts in the program were not exactly bad." In fact, probably due to the real aerial engagement he had witnessed, Ernst August upon his departure left behind three of his Duchy's War Merit Crosses, 2nd Class – and two of them went to Buddecke and Althaus.[17]

During the summer of 1915, *Hptm.* Erich Serno was given permission to expand the *Fliegertruppe's* presence in Turkey and among other things, form a *Fokkerstaffel* (a unit consisting of Fokker fighters) at the Dardanelles.[18] Buddecke volunteered his services – perhaps again because "an opportunity was offered... to go out into the world and see a bit

of it" – and was accepted that winter.[19] All officers who served in the German Military Mission in Turkey were temporarily advanced one rank by their hosts. Thus in December 1915, now as a *Hauptmann* with three victories to his credit (his third had fallen on 11 November), Buddecke journeyed by train from Berlin to Vienna, then to Budapest and over Bulgaria to Constantinople (now Istanbul), where he arrived on the 13th. Then an automobile carried him to a hill near Uzunköprü where a new air base was situated: "Air base. In reality, a house made of boards was there and a hangar had been built. That was all." He and another pilot, Hans Schüz, spent Christmas there and then moved south to Galata (now Sütlüce) on the Gallipoli peninsula where they were joined by *Lt.* Theodor Croneiss and *Lt.* Erich Muhra (*Oberleutnants* in the Turkish military). Their small unit (two Fokker E.IIIs, one Fokker E.II and possibly one Fokker E.I) was officially designated as Turkish *Flieger-Abteilung* 6 and Buddecke was placed in command.

Buddecke drew first blood when he downed two Farmans on 6 January 1916 – one confirmed, one unconfirmed.[20] As with many of the claims made by both sides in the Turkish theater, accurate information has been difficult to obtain. Several modern sources have given the location of Buddecke's first 6 January victory as east of "Cape Narors." British records tell us that a Flt. Cdr. Hans Acworth Busk (No.2 Naval Wing RNAS) went missing that day so it has often been assumed that Busk was Buddecke's confirmed victim. Buddecke's second victory of 6 January is said to have occurred east of Jalova, with little more detail. The following

14

Left & Below: Heinz Nowarra identified the first picture as an *Esc*. MF 98.T Maurice Farman brought down by Buddecke. If so, it may have been Baptiste de Conte's on 6 January 1916. Alternatively, it could have been one of Buddecke's 25 or 27 January victories about which very little is known. The second picture, published in a Turkish newspaper, shows the same plane being visited by various military officials.

سطح البحر اوزرنده طیاره‌مزك آچدیغی بر محاربه‌ هوائیه‌ نتیجه‌سنده‌ مغلوب بار به‌ اینن بر دشمن طیاره‌سنك عاقبتی

review of previously unpublished information gives us a clearer picture, however. First we have Cenk Avci's report in his book, *The Skies of Gallipoli*: "On January 6, the Allied aeroplanes raided Galata airbase but they failed to cause any damage to the camp. Air Lieutenant Buddecke responded promptly and took off from the airbase and shot down one French Farman aeroplane under the control of pilot Leconte. She crashed on the Asiatic side between the Ozbek and Karacaviran district. Leconte died in the crash. On the afternoon of the same day, Buddecke again shot down another Allied aeroplane in the Burhani area with his Fokker." This is supported by a relatively unknown article in the wartime newspaper, *Kriegs-Chronik der Leipziger Neuesten Nachrichten*, which stated: "*6.Januar 1916.*

Leutnant Buddecke (*Oberleutnant der Reserve des Leibgarderegiments 115 Hermann Buddecke, der als Hauptmann der deutschen Militärmission angehört) griff ein französisches Flugzeug, das die Meerenge überflog, an, beschädigte es und brachte es an der anatolischen Küste dicht bei Akbaschi zum Absturz. Das feindliche Flugzeug wird leicht wieder hergestellt werden können. Der französische Flieger wurde tot aufgefunden."* ("6 January 1916. *Leutnant* Buddecke (*Oberleutnant d.R.* of Body Guard Regiment 115 Hermann Buddecke, who is a *Hauptmann* in the German Military Mission) attacked a French airplane that flew over the strait, damaged it and caused it to crash on the Anatoli Coast close by Akbaschi. The enemy airplane was easily repaired. The French airman was found dead.")[21] Quite fortuitously, a member of the Great War Forum website shared a period photograph published on a postcard entitled "British and French graves at Cape Helles Gallipoli" that among its subjects displayed a grave cross with the following German inscription: *"Hier ruht ..?.. französische Flieger Baptiste de Conte gefallen im Luftkampf am 6. January 1916."* ("Here lies ..?.. French airman Baptiste de Conte, killed in air combat on 6 January 1916.").[22] We know that French *Escadrille* MF 98.T ("T" for Tenedos, where it was based) flew Farmans and other types in support of British efforts at the Dardanelles, and it seems likely that Baptiste de Conte belonged to that unit. *Kriegs-Chronik der Leipziger Neuesten Nachrichten* reported Buddecke's second victory of 6 January the following day: *"7.Januar 1916. An der Dardanellenfront griff das von Leutnant Buddecke geführte Flugzeug außer dem feindlichen Flugzeug, dessen Sturz wir gestern meldeten, noch ein zweites feindliches Flugzeug an, das brennend abstürzte. Das erste dieser Flugzeuge ist ein französisches, Typ Farman Nr.42 und fiel am 6.Januar vormittags östlich des Kap Nagara; das andere, ein englisches, Typ Farman, fiel auf die europäische Küste östlich von Jalova."* ("7 January 1916. On the Dardanelle Front, *Leutnant* Buddecke, who got an enemy airplane whose crash we reported yesterday, also attacked a second airplane that fell burning. The first of these planes was French, a Farman Nr.42 type that fell on the morning of 6 January east of Cape Nagara. The second, an English Farman type, fell on the European coast east of Jalova.") Hans Busk's friend, Flt. Lt. Theophilus Chater Vernon, wrote that: "Hans went out on Jan 6th in a Henry Farman biplane with a 130hp engine... he started off at about 3pm carrying a 550lb bomb... on account of the great weight he naturally went alone. As Hans carried no observer he therefore carried no gun, and was last seen about 5 miles by

air from the Gelata Aerodrome (German)."[23] Taken together, all the evidence points to Buddecke first bringing down *Esc.* MF 98.T's Baptiste de Conte between Ozbek (now Özbek) and Karacaviran (now Karacaören), just east of Cape Nara (not Narors)[24]. De Conte's Farman was salvaged and his body probably buried nearby. Sometime later, the contents of his grave and its marker (with its German inscription) were transferred to a site near Helles where other Frenchmen were interred alongside their British colleagues.[25] The Germans undoubtedly had a plane and a body, so de Conte most likely was Buddecke's confirmed victory of 6 January. Buddecke then shot down No.2 Naval Wing's Hans Busk "in the Burhani area" later that afternoon. Modern-day Burhanli is on the Dardanelles coast, east of Jalova (now Yalova) within five miles of Buddecke's Galata (Sütlüce) base. It is possible that "in the area" meant that the plane and pilot both went down offshore. If so, then there was no body or aircraft and the victory therefore went unconfirmed.

Kriegs-Chronik der Leipziger Neuesten Nachrichten published several other pertinent reports such as the following (translated into English): "9 January 1916. One of our airmen attacked an enemy Farman-type biplane that went down, enveloped in flames, near Seddülbahir." "12 January 1916. Our aircraft, piloted by *Leutnants* Buddecke and Chonos [SIC – Croneiss], shot down a fourth enemy airman on 9 January. He crashed into the open sea near Seddülbahir." "13 January 1916. On the afternoon of 12 January, an airplane piloted by Buddecke attacked a fifth Farman-type enemy airplane and caused it to crash in the vicinity of Seddülbahir. We discovered that the pilot was dead, the observer wounded. The airplane became useable after minor repairs." As before, the Buddecke/Croneiss victory on 9 January went unconfirmed since the plane disappeared into the sea. Buddecke's 12 January success was upheld, however, because the plane and its crew fell into German hands. According to Henshaw, the victims would have been Flt. Sub-Lt. J.S. Bolas and Midshipman D.M. Branson of either No.2 or No.3 Naval Wing RNAS.[26] In between, on 11 January, both Buddecke and Schüz claimed Farmans brought down near Seddülbahir. Schüz's was upheld, Buddecke's was not (probably because it went down into the sea). Henshaw notes that two RNAS pilots were lost that day: Flt. Sub-Lt. C.H. Brimstead and Flt. Lt. N.H. Boles, both killed in action.[27]

Buddecke was granted two more confirmed victories on 25 and 27 January. Henshaw lists no British losses for those dates and the *Kriegs-Chronik der Leipziger Neuesten Nachrichten* only reported:

An artist's conception of "*Hauptmann* Buddecke, the successful Fokker flyer" and his victory over a French airplane near the Dardanelles. Buddecke was fortunate that his fighter, unlike this drawing of it, was armed with a machine gun.

"29 January 1916. The Milli Agency announces: airman *Oblt*. Buddecke caused several enemy aircraft to crash on the Dardanelles." Thus the identities of these victims are unknown.

It was around this time that Buddecke reported to Enver Pasha, Turkey's Minister of War, somewhere on Gallipoli's battlefield.[28] Buddecke described how after a brief discussion, the War Minister took a Golden Liakat Medal from one of his adjutant's hands and pinned it on him, saying: "This is not a reward, only a little memento."[29] In recognition of his successes, Buddecke's Turkish admirers also gave him the sobriquet, "*El Schahin*" ("The Falcon"), which he later used for the title of his short autobiography.[30]

Kriegs-Chronik der Leipziger Neuesten Nachrichten had this to say about Buddecke's next two claims on 30 March and 4 April: "1 April 1916. On 30 March, two of our aircraft under the command of *Hptm*. Boedge [SIC – Buddecke] attacked enemy airmen that flew over Seddülbahir. During the air combat, one of the enemy airplanes fell into the sea while the others fled toward Imbros [now Gökçeada]." "8 April 1916. On 4 April eight enemy aircraft flew over Gallipoli peninsula. *Hptm*. Buddecke attacked them with his airplane, and during the course of the air battle caused one enemy plane to crash outside of Kumdere. The plane immediately sank into the sea. Investigating enemy torpedo boats, which rushed to help, were unsuccessful." Regarding this 4 April fight, Buddecke himself related: "I spotted a bright-colored gentleman under me. I was on him in a flash. I aimed well after three spirals – he tipped over, plunged, his wings folded up together, he fell into the sea. English torpedo boats came to fish him out."[31] Once again, both claims were lost at sea, evidently preventing their official confirmation.

Buddecke was then granted what he called "*der blaue Max*" ("the Blue Max") on 14 April 1916 when

A portion of this photograph was published in the 27 February 1916 edition of *Illustrierte Kriegs-Zeitung* (82, p.3), so we know it was taken soon after Buddecke's receipt of the Golden Liakat Medal (visible above his Iron Cross, 1st Class). Though dressed in his Turkish uniform, his Prussian Pilot's Badge is displayed on his tunic.

his official tally stood at seven.[32] Considerable attention has been paid above to Buddecke's victory claims because he evidently did not meet the *Orden Pour le Mérite* eligibility standard applied to Boelcke, Immelmann and ten other pilots after him – that is, eight confirmed victories. In light of the information just reviewed, it is understandable if those who submitted and accepted Buddecke's recommendation for the decoration felt he deserved it nonetheless. If not for the sea swallowing up necessary evidence, Buddecke might have been credited with eight as early as 12 January 1916 (just like Boelcke and Immelmann). Moreover, the majority of his successes had been achieved in a theater of operations that offered fewer opportunities than those on the Western Front. All in all, it is difficult to dispute the argument that Hans-Joachim Buddecke's record at that time merited the slight exception that was apparently made in his case.

Shortly after his receipt of the *Pour le Mérite*, Buddecke went back to Germany on leave. He

A candid shot of Buddecke relaxing in a chair.

may not have spent much of it at his home, however. One photograph (below) tells us that he was with his former unit, *FFA* 23, at Vaux on 7 May. Oswald Boelcke wrote that Buddecke "told me some very interesting tales" the next day at German Headquarters at Charleville.[33] There are snapshots of Buddecke with several members of *Kampfgeschwader (KG)* 1 while others show him visiting with Anthony Fokker. Whether on official or unofficial business, he clearly made the rounds. While doing so, he proudly wore his Turkish *Hauptmann's* uniform (complete with Kalpak hat), augmented by his Golden Liakat Medal and *Pour le Mérite*.

After his return to Turkey, Buddecke left Turkish *FA* 6 to head a small fighter unit based at Smyrna (now Izmir); and it was there, at the city's railway station, that he greeted Oswald Boelcke on 20 July 1916 during the latter's tour of the Balkans, Turkey and the Eastern Front. Buddecke entertained Boelcke for several days and even arranged a yachting party where the men and women went swimming in the bay. On 25 July, Boelcke wrote: "I now have to go

Above: The duty board in the background tells us that this picture of Buddecke's visit to his former unit, *FFA 23*, occurred on 7 May 1916. *FFA 23*'s CO, *Hptm*. Karl Seber, stands to the right of Buddecke; and the man to the right of Seber is *Oblt*. Friedrich Schüler van Krieken. Other men who can be identified: *Lt*. Walter Gnamm (third from left), *Hptm*. Eberhard Bohnstedt (fourth from left), *Lt*. Hans-Joachim von Seydlitz-Gerstenberg (behind and to the left of Buddecke), *Lt*. Walter Sieber (between Buddecke and Seber), *Lt*. Grüner (above Seber), *Oblt*. Jakob von Hartsen (between Seber and Krieken), *Oblt*. Souchy (above Krieken), *Lt*. Erwin Tütschulte (third from right), and *Lt*. Böhmer (second from right).

Facing Page: Buddecke also visited *KG* 1 during his leave. These two photos were taken then with the first showing Buddecke flanked by the unit's CO, *Hptm*. Ernst von Gersdorf (right), and *Hptm*. Julius Schulz. The second has Gersdorf in the middle with future *Pour le Mérite* holder *Hptm*. Rudolf Kleine at right. Gersdorff was killed within weeks of these snapshots, apparently by *Escadrille* N57 ace Jean Chaput, on 19 June. (first photo courtesy of Tobias Weber)

Left: Buddecke and *Oblt*. Friedrich Schüler van Krieken pose in front of one of *FFA 23*'s observation planes at another time during Buddecke's spring 1916 leave (their outfits are different than those seen above). Krieken joined Buddecke in Turkey the following June and subsequently became the Turkish Fifth Army's Aviation Staff Officer.

Above: Anthony Fokker (left), *Hptm*. Albert Mühlig-Hofmann (center) and Buddecke stand in front of what was probably Fokker's D.I prototype, 140/16, at Schwerin sometime during his leave. A portion of this picture was later used in advertisements by propeller manufacturer Garuda.

Above & Right: Two more portraits of Buddecke taken during his spring 1916 leave in Germany.

Above: *Gen.* Liman von Sanders (center) had this photo taken of himself with Buddecke (left) and *Hptm.* Oswald Boelcke on 20 July 1916 during Boelcke's visit to Turkey. Buddecke is now wearing the larger Golden Imtiaz Medal on his chest.

the long way round by Constantinople to the Dardanelles. I could have been there in two and a half hours in an aeroplane, but Buddecke will not let me have one. He gave me a thousand reasons why it was impossible, but I believe he received instuctions from the air chief or even from G.H.Q. that I must not fly here either."[34] A picture taken of Buddecke and Boelcke on 20 July is the first time we see Buddecke adorned with the Golden Imtiaz Medal, which Hanns Möller claimed was given to him by the Sultan of Turkey, Mohammed V.[35] Evidently, Buddecke had received it sometime in June or early July.

When the new *Jagdstaffel* system was implemented in August 1916, Buddecke left Turkey and was given command of *Jasta* 4 – a unit with his former *FFA* 23's *KEK* Vaux at its core. It was a talented group that not only included four recent *Pour le Mérite* recipients (Kurt Wintgens – 1 July, Walter Höhndorf – 20 July, Ernst von Althaus – 21 July, Wilhelm Frankl – 12 August) but three future ones as well (Rudolf Berthold – 12 October 1916, Fritz Otto Bernert – 23 April 1917, Josef Veltjens – 16 August 1918).[36]

Buddecke led by example and shot three planes down in September, bringing his official total to 10. Only five pilots had a better record at that point: the great Oswald Boelcke (29), the late Max Immelmann (15), Kurt Wintgens (19), Wilhelm Frankl (13) and Walter Höhndorf (12).

The precise identification of World War I pilot claims has always been a challenge to modern historians, and Buddecke's September victories are no exception. *Jasta* 4's war diary states that Buddecke's eighth – a "Vikkers" near Chaulnes – fell on 16 September 1916. Yet the five FE.2b aircraft ("Vikkers" was a term that German airmen often

generically applied to any British lattice-tailed plane) reported as having been downed or damaged that day were not in the vicinity of Chaulnes.[37] Then we have Buddecke's ninth on 22 September. Most historians agree that it was FE.2b 4937 of RFC No.18 Squadron because it was listed as having gone down near Ginchy and Buddecke's claim was near Combles (within two miles of Ginchy). Yet photographic evidence first presented by this author in another work and now supported by information from the Tobias Weber collection suggests something else. Several photos exist of FE.2b 6937 – another RFC No.18 Squadron plane brought down and captured during the same engagement – at *Jasta* 4's Roupy airfield. In one of them, Buddecke is standing near the tail as if to indicate that it was his conquest. Two other pictures of the same FE.2b at Roupy have been found among Buddecke's personal records, and on the back of one he wrote that he had forced it to land near Nesle (south of Péronne). He also said that its crew had consisted of an Englishman and an Anglo-American from California, both of whom were wounded, and that the plane bore two labels: "Punjab Rawalpindi" and "Dolores la Vivandière" – certain attributes of 6937.[38] Was this his actual ninth victim or was it another that was, despite having been captured, not officially awarded to him? To confuse matters further, Buddecke identified it as his eleventh victory.[39] Only Buddecke's tenth official victory, downed the next day on 23 September, seems to have a fairly certain identification.

Above: Three candid snapshots of Buddecke when he was in command of *Jasta* 4. Two of them include *Lt.* Walter Höhndorf (right) as well. (first photo courtesy of Greg VanWyngarden)

The *Pour le Mérite* "club" was severely shaken when Kurt Wintgens was killed in action on 25 September. Rudolf Berthold scored his eighth victory the next day on 26 September and was duly awarded the *Pour le Mérite* on 12 October 1916. As several photos attest, *Jasta* 4 threw him a celebratory party. But *Jasta* 4's fortunes waned for the rest of the year, for after having scored 15 victories in September, it managed to bring down only four in October, three in November and none in December.[40]

In the fall of 1916, Enver Pasha had gained the approval of his German allies to expand the air forces in Turkey to 100 aircraft in 1917. The Turkish Air Service was reorganized into the Turkish *Luftstreitkräfte* (air force) with an independent command structure and offices at military headquarters in Istanbul (formerly Constantinople). Commanded by *Hptm.* Erich Serno (a *Major* in the Turkish service), it was identified as *Abteilung* 13

and based at a hotel in Pera (now Beyoglu), a suburb of Istanbul.[41] Serno was promised more German officers and technical staff as a result; and no doubt

Buddecke poses in front of FE.2b 6937 after it had been taken to *Jasta* 4's Roupy airfield.

Facing Page & Above: The first photo captures the men of *Jasta* 4 and guests celebrating *Oblt*. Rudolf Berthold's *Pour le Mérite* bestowal on 12 October 1916. Seated in chairs (left to right): unknown, *Lt*. Walter Höhndorf, *Lt*. Alfred Lenz, unknown, Berthold, Buddecke, *Lt*. Wilhelm Frankl, *Oblt*. Ernst von Althaus. Standing behind them are *Lt*. Walter Gnamm and *Vzfw*. Josef Veltjens, third and fourth from the left, and *Lt*. Fritz Otto Bernert, fourth from the right. The next two were taken around the same time. In the second, left to right: Lenz, *Lt*. Karl Stehle, Höhndorf, *Vzfw*. Hermann Margot, Buddecke, *Lt*. Krawleski, Berthold, Bernert, Althaus, *Lt*. Hans Malchow, Frankl. Third, left to right: Bernert, Stehle, Althaus, Frankl, Buddecke, Lenz, Malchow, Berthold, Höhndorf.

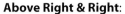

Above Right & Right: Two poorer quality photos of Buddecke and *Oblt*. Friedrich Schüler van Krieken together again in Turkey. The first is the only known picture of Buddecke wearing both the Golden and Silver Imtiaz Medals on his chest. The second has, from left to right: Krieken, *Maj*. Erich Serno, Buddecke, and *Hptm*. Shakir Feyzi Bey (Serno's Chief of Staff) at Smyrna.

Above & Below: These pictures come from a series taken at *Jasta* 18's quarters near Avelin within a few days of Buddecke's death. In the front row of the first (left to right): *Vzfw*. Hermann Margot, *Lt*. Hugo Schäfer, *Lt*. Hans von Buttlar, *Lt*. Josef Veltjens, *Hptm*. Rudolf Berthold, *Lt*. Walther Kleffel, Buddecke, *Lt*. Johannes Klein, *Lt*. Oliver von Beaulieu-Marconnay, *Lt*. Arthur Rahn. The back row (left to right): *Lt*. Georg von Hantelmann, *Lt*. P. Lohmann, *Oblt*. Ernst Wilhelm Turck, *Lt*. Walter Dingel, *Vzfw*. Theodor Weischer. (photos courtesy of Arthur Rahn album via Terry Phillips)

as part of this commitment, Hans-Joachim Buddecke was asked to return to Turkey, which he did in mid-December 1916. Initially, he was placed in charge of Turkish *FA* 5's fighter contingent based at Sevdi-köi (now Sevgi), south of Smyrna (now Izmir). Then his territory was expanded, as he put it, "about 100 kilometers further northward."[42] This would explain one of Buddecke's calling cards, now in a private collection, that lists the title *"Hauptmann u. Chef der Flieger auf Gallipoli u. Klein-Asien"* ("Captain and Chief of Airmen at Gallipoli and Asia Minor") along with the address *"Constantinopel Gr. H.-Qu. Abt. 13"* ("Constantinople Supreme Headquarters Section 13"). Buddecke's small fighter group was charged with the responsibility of defending the western coast of Turkey from Smyrna up to Gallipoli. Because it had to roam between coastal airbases as the situation demanded, he dubbed it *"Der Wanderzirkus"* ("The Traveling Circus").[43]

The English flew several sorties over Smyrna in late March 1917. In response, Buddecke went there on the 27th, hid his plane and waited. On 30 March, he was notified that three enemy aircraft were headed toward the city. He took off, climbed and managed to get above Henri Farman F27 N3024 of No.2 Wing RNAS, manned by Flt. Sub-Lt. B.A. Trechmann (pilot) and Leading Midshipman W.A. Jones. He immediately dove onto their tail and shot until the plane's propeller stopped, causing it to fall. Then he heard another noise: "Something rattles behind me. I turn. A Nieuport from above. Directly underneath him, I climb toward him. He lets up from his attack, starts again, I pivot in his direction... I calmly press the small tab on the steering column. My guns work. My opponent's right wing breaks away, and he falls."[44] He had gotten No.2 Wing's Nieuport 12 9203, crewed by Flt. Lt. J.E. Morgan (pilot) and Flt. Sub-Lt. A Sandell. The third plane flew away. In recognition of the event, the citizens of Smyrna gave him a gold plaque upon which the dogfight was depicted. Sometime during this second tour of Turkey, Buddecke decided upon an important commitment. He put in for full reinstatement in the military (as opposed to reserve status) and was granted it in 1917.

According to Serno's memoirs, Buddecke was given a railway freight car in settlement of a gambling debt. At some point in early 1918, he got into trouble with Turkish authorities when he sold it to a Jewish merchant. It was then that Buddecke requested a transfer back to the Western Front[45]. Germany was preparing for its great spring offensive in the west, "Operation Michael," so the *Luftstreitkräfte* was probably all too happy to gain the services of an experienced combat pilot toward that effort. Buddecke, with 12 official victories to his credit, departed from Turkey in early February 1918 and began his tenure with *Jasta* 30 on the 15th. He was not placed in command, however, and took on the duties of an ordinary line pilot. This may have been due to any one or more of the following reasons: it was a punitive action stemming from the controversy in Turkey, he needed familiarization with the aircraft and tactics of the Western Front, the unit's current CO (*Oblt.* Hans Bethge) was more senior and more successful with a victory tally of 18. Whatever the circumstances, Buddecke proved his mettle just four days later when he and Bethge gunned down two Sopwith Camels and damaged a third during a fight with RFC No.80 Squadron on 19 February. It was Buddecke's 13th and would be his last of the war.

Buddecke's old friend from *FFA* 23 and *Jasta* 4, Rudolf Berthold, had been severely wounded in the right arm on 10 October 1917. Months later, it was still healing and Berthold, CO of *Jasta* 18, remained unable to lead his men in the air. So it is said that he asked Buddecke to join his unit to help him in this capacity. Before this, Berthold had written: "To me, Buddecke was the dearest of comrades. Loyal and honest, he is adventurous up to the point of being a daredevil; tough and ruthless when it comes to himself, he nevertheless is full of feelings and so modest. We have always stuck by each other faithfully and will always remain good friends in the future."[46] Buddecke arrived at *Jasta* 18 on 8 March and posed with its men in several photographs that marked the event. It is clear that their spirits were high that day. The reverie ended just two days later, however, when a flight from *Jasta* 18, led by Buddecke, tangled with a group of Sopwith Camels from RNAS No.3 Squadron. It appears that Buddecke was bested by eventual 27-victory ace Capt. Arthur T. Whealy. Whealy wrote: "I dived down with my flight on about seven or eight enemy aircraft. After pulling out of a dive on one enemy aircraft I saw another to my left about 500 ft. below, heading away from me. I immediately dived on his tail and opened fire at about 100 yards, firing a burst of about 40 rounds from each gun. The enemy aircraft turned half over onto its back and went down in a series of stalls and spins. I watched it till it was about 3000–4000 ft. above the ground and then lost sight of it on account of the haze, but I feel fairly certain that I hit the pilot. Other pilots of the patrol observed the enemy aircraft crash."[47] The afterword to Buddecke's autobiography states that he had been shot through the heart.

A memorial ceremony was held for Buddecke near

Hans-Joachim Buddecke's coffin is carried from a Berlin chapel on its way to the city's Invalidenfriedhof cemetery.

Jasta 18's base at Avelin, after which his body was placed on a train for transport back to Germany. On 22 March, Buddecke's remains were lowered into their final resting place at Berlin's Invalidenfriedhof cemetery.

Endnotes

[1] He was buried next to his son, Hans-Joachim, in Berlin's Invalidenfriedhof cemetery.
[2] U.S. patent 1,708,869 was awarded to him on 9 April 1929.
[3] *El Schahin*, p.9.
[4] *El Schahin*, p.10.
[5] *El Schahin*, p.11.
[6] *El Schahin*, p.23.
[7] *El Schahin*, p.24.
[8] *El Schahin*, p.30.
[9] *El Schahin*, p.33.
[10] *El Schahin*, p.43.
[11] Ibid.
[12] "Full-fuselaged" was used here to distinguish the BE.2c from the lattice-tailed aircraft (e.g., Maurice Farman, Voisin, FE.2, DH.2) often flown at the time.
[13] Buddecke presumably used this analogy because the peacock butterfly sports four distinct roundels on its wings.
[14] *El Schahin*, pp.45–50.
[15] For this and the day's account in its entirety, see *El Schahin*, pp.51–63. Did 'Mumm' refer to another member of *FFA* 23 or to the famous champagne produced by G.H. Mumm & Co.? The royal visitors

were Ernst August, Duke of Brunswick and August Wilhelm, Prince of Prussia. For Schüler, see footnote 19.
[16] Buddecke related three particularly interesting details in his description of the fight. First, he stated that before opening fire from 50 meters distance he "put his head against the rest, his eye firmly on the sight and bead" – a relatively rare reference to the aiming head rests sometimes seen in photos of early *Eindecker* models. Second, he related that BE.2 gas fumes had a unique odor that "was sweeter than a lace handkerchief" and would stay in his nose for days afterwards. Third, he mentioned that *FFA* 23's CO (*Hptm.* Karl Seber) quickly cordoned off the crash site denying access "in particular to the airmen officers of the *Abteilung*." Presumably, the reason was to spare them from seeing first hand what could happen to them.
[17] Neal O'Connor (*Aviation Awards of Imperial Germany 7*, pp. 46–47) speculated that the third War Merit Cross went to *FFA* 23 CO Karl Seber.
[18] Serno was one of Germany's early pre-war pilots, having earned German Pilot's License No.301 on 9 October 1912.
[19] Buddecke mentioned that his good friend from *FFA* 23, "observer Schüler," who had also volunteered for duty with the German Military Mission in Turkey, had been turned down. This was *Oblt.* Friedrich Schüler van Krieken, who finally made it to Turkey in June 1916 and was appointed (with Buddecke's help?) *Stabsoffizier der Flieger* (Aviation Staff Officer) for the Turkish 5th

Army in August.

[20] Sources often list a prior unconfirmed victory on 6 December 1915 for Buddecke (e.g., Franks, Bailey and Guest, *Above the Lines*, p.88); but this seems virtually impossible given Buddecke's own account of his arrival in Turkey well after that date.

[21] Why the newspaper ranked him as a *Leutnant* when it also explained his status as a German *Oberleutnant* and Turkish *Hauptmann* is a mystery. It also mistakenly reported his first name as "Hermann." This and other of the newspaper's accounts are also available on the Australian Flying Corps 1914–1919 website: http://www.southsearepublic.org/2002_1999/afc_documents_turkishreports_dardanelles_1916.htm

[22] See website: http://1914-1918.invisionzone.com/forums/index.php?showtopic=25419&st=0.

[23] For this and more on Flt. Cdr. Busk, see the website: http://www.rudgwickremembers.co.uk/Men%20WW1/Busk%20Hans%20Acworth/Hans%20Acworth%20Busk.htm

[24] This writer was unable to identify an "Akbaschi" in Turkey or anything similar to it between Özbek and Karacaören on modern maps.

[25] After the war, the British consolidated many of their countrymen's graves at the Helles Memorial whereas the French consolidated theirs just north of nearby Morto Bay.

[26] Henshaw, *The Sky Their Battlefield*, p.496. [Grub Street, 1995]

[27] Ibid.

[28] The 12 February 1916 edition of *Die Woche* (7, p.227) announced that he had won the "*Goldenen Liakatmedaille*" for recent actions over the Dardanelles.

[29] *El Schahin*, p.89.

[30] The caption under Buddecke's photo in the 12 February 1916 edition of *Die Woche* (7, p.227) states this.

[31] *El Schahin*, p.84. Henshaw (see above) reports no British losses for these dates.

[32] *El Schahin*, p.91.

[33] Werner, *Knight of Germany*, p.167; Werner, *Boelcke: der Mensch*, p.153. [Prof. Johannes Werner *Boelcke: der Mensch* (Verlag K.F. Koehler, 1932)] [Prof. Johannes Werner (trans. by Claud Sykes), *Knight of Germany* (Greenhill Books, 1985)]

[34] Werner, *Knight of Germany*, p.195; *Werner, Boelcke: der Mensch*, p.177. Boelcke had been temporarily grounded and sent on his tour following the death of Max Immelmann on 18 June 1916.

[35] Möller, *Geschichte der Ritter des Ordens "Pour le Mérite"* 1, p.168.

[36] Though some historians place Wintgens and Höhndorf at *Jasta* 1 in early September, numerous photos and Buddecke's specific statement that *Jasta* 4 started out with five *Pour le Mérite* holders including them attest to their being with *Jasta* 4 during its early weeks (see *El Schahin*, pp.92–93). Wintgens and Höhndorf were probably transferred to *Jasta* 1 later that month shortly before Wintgens was killed on 25 September.

[37] The other aircraft shot up that day – two BE.2c's and one Morane LA – were not lattice-tailed and were not involved in engagements anywhere near Chaulnes.

[38] These match the details provided by The Royal Air Force Museum and Cross & Cockade, *FE2b/d*, pp.137–38.

[39] It was not uncommon for pilots to include unofficial victories in their personal total.

[40] Compare this to *Jasta* 2's 32 victories in October, 25 in November and 10 in December. Hans von Keudell of *Jasta* 1 partly blamed *Jasta* 2's success for scaring off the enemy, stating in an 8 October 1916 letter that "our game has been terribly spooked. Boelcke is just too great a gunner." (O'Connor, *Aviation Awards of Imperial Germany 6*, p.316). Nevertheless, Keudell alone – who shot down nine planes in October–November 1916 – did better than *Jasta* 4.

[41] *Hptm*. Shakir Feyzi Bey, a close supporter of *Hptm*. Erich Serno, was appointed Chief of Staff of the *Luftstreitkräfte*.

[42] *El Schahin*, p.107.

[43] *El Schahin*, p.106.

[44] *El Schahin*, p.113.

[45] See O'Connor, *Aviation Awards of Imperial Germany 7*, p.52.

[46] Gengler, *Kampfflieger Rudolf Berthold*, p.48.

[47] VanWyngarden, *Jasta 18*, p.63.

Buddecke and Anthony Fokker standing in front of a Fokker E.IV.

Buddecke – The Aircraft

Unfortunately, Hans-Joachim Buddecke had very little to say in his autobiography, *El Schahin (der Jagdfalke)*, about the various aircraft he flew throughout his career. Therefore, the following information for the most part is based on photographs from the Tobias Weber collection and other independent records.

Nieuport (IV?) Monoplane
(Spring–July 1914)

Buddecke stated that he taught himself how to fly in a Nieuport monoplane that he bought in Chicago in the spring of 1914. A photo of the plane, B1, was included in his autobiography; and thanks to Tobias Weber, we also have B2, a picture of Buddecke in front of the same Nieuport. It appears to have been a Nieuport IV, first produced in 1911. This identification is somewhat uncertain, however, because Buddecke said it was powered by a 35 hp Gnome engine and the Nieuport IV normally came with a 50 hp rotary (an engine that Buddecke indeed upgraded to before flying his Nieuport). He continued to fly this airplane until news of the war reached him.

B1–2. The Nieuport monoplane around which Hans-Joachim Buddecke built his short-lived American airplane company in 1914. Buddecke is standing just behind the wing in B2. (second photo courtesy of Tobias Weber)

LVG B.I, Albatros B.I
(September 1914–August 1915)

Buddecke said nothing about the types of two-seat reconnaissance and fighting machines he flew while with *Ettapen-Flugzeug-Park 2*, *FFA 27* and *FFA 23*. Still, photos in the Tobias Weber collection give us a glimpse of some of them. B3 has Buddecke and some of his *EFP 2* comrades next to an Albatros B.I. B4 is a snapshot of him posing in front of an LVG B.I. B5–6 capture him and one of his observers in *FFA 23*, *Lt.* Trentepohl, in and alongside an Albatros B.I.[1] These aircraft were prewar types that were adapted for reconnaissance and training duties during the early months of the war.

B3. Buddecke stands in company with two veteran, pre-war fliers and other *EFP 2* colleagues alongside one of its Albatros B.I planes. Left to right: Buddecke, Ernst Schlegel (German Pilot's License No.209, awarded on 20 May 1912), *Fw.* Oscar Wittenstein (Pilot's License No.81, awarded on 29 April 1911), *Lt.* Rudolf Berthold, *Lt.* Beck. (photo courtesy of Tobias Weber)

B4. Buddecke and an LVG B.I that he presumably flew early during his career. (photo courtesy of Tobias Weber)

B5–6. Buddecke earned his Pilot's Badge while serving with *FFA* 27 before his transfer to *FFA* 23 in the summer of 1915. These two pictures show him when he was an Albatros B.I pilot in *FFA* 23 with *Lt*. Trentepohl as his observer. Before the advent of the armed C-type biplanes, pilots normally occupied the rear cockpit. (photos courtesy of Tobias Weber)

Fokker E.I 15/15, E.II 36/15 (Late August–November 1915)

In late August 1915, Buddecke got to fly a Fokker *Eindecker* that had been assigned to *FFA* 23, based near Vaux. At this point in the war, it could only have been an E.I or E.II because the E.III did not arrive at the Front in any numbers until November

B7–10. Buddecke and his first Fokker *Eindecker*, E.I 15/15, at *FFA* 23's base near Saint-Quentin. (photos courtesy of Tobias Weber)

B11. Two ground crewmen prepare *FFA* 23's other *Eindecker*, E.II 36/15, for takeoff. (photo courtesy of Greg VanWyngarden)

1915.[2] B7–10 are previously unpublished pictures of what was unquestionably the first *Eindecker* he flew with *FFA* 23 – E.I 15/15, one of Fokker's first batch of fighters. Buddecke related that after his departure to Turkey, Ernst von Althaus inherited "my Fokker" and that it was in turn passed along to Berthold.[3] This means that it was kept in service throughout Buddecke's tenure at *FFA* 23. After Berthold, E.I 15/15 was given over to the German Navy's *Kampfeinsitzer Schule* (single-seat fighter plane school) at Mannheim-Sandhofen.[4]

B11 is a picture of Buddecke in a Fokker E.II whose serial number appears to have been 36/15. This has at times been called into question because an E.I with the same serial number reportedly arrived in Gallipoli, Turkey in September 1915.[5] However, a recent photo discovery that will be presented in the next volume in this series confirms that Buddecke was sitting in 36/15 and that it was the second of *FFA* 23's two Fokkers that was flown by Ernst von Althaus. B11 demonstrates that Buddecke flew it on occasion as well. Still, B7–10 and Buddecke's narrative suggest that he considered E.I 15/15 to be his principal mount during his stay with *FFA* 23 (i.e., up through November 1915).

Fokker E.III (96/15, 108/15 or both) (January–early August 1916)

Buddecke came to Turkey in late December 1915. Shortly before, three Fokker aircraft had been delivered to the Gallipoli Front where he was headed: E.III 108/15 (F 2 in Turkish army records), E.III 96/15 (F 3) and E.II 93/15 (F 4).[6] They formed the core of his *Fokkerstaffel*, which consisted of "three

pilots, six mechanics and an interpreter."[7] B12 and B13 are pictures of Buddecke in front of E.III 96/15, presumably at his unit's Galata airfield. This does not necessarily prove that he personally flew it, but it does seems likely that he, as the unit's CO, would have flown at least one of the newer E.IIIs. Buddecke described his *Eindecker* as "my yellow bird with black, threatening eyes on the wingtips – one to the right, one to the left."[8] The *Eindecker*'s standard, clear-doped linen covering had a yellow cast to it, and the "eyes" were the black squares outlined in white that served as the national insignia on Turkish aircraft. B14 is a well-known picture of Buddecke in front of another Turkish-marked E.III (the type number is visible on the fuselage just to the left of Buddecke).[9] Its darker appearance compared to B12–13 has led many authorities to reasonably speculate that it had been painted gray, green or brown – similar to what appears to have been the case for Turkey's later Halberstadt fighters. Yet we now have ample evidence that the color yellow could be represented by various shades in the orthochrome film used at the time, i.e., anywhere from light to dark gray. Some pictures of natural-wood Albatros fighters in Turkey, perhaps because of the bright sunlight, gave them a very dark appearance as well. If one looks at the shades of the men's skins in B14, they are similarly quite dark. Though we may never know the answer, it is at least possible that the Eindecker in B14 was clear-doped too.

Replacement aircraft were very difficult to obtain in Turkey, so Buddecke presumably scored most or all of his victories during the period January–April 1916 in one or both of these aircraft.

B12–13. Buddecke (just right of center, wearing tropical helmet) stands near E.III 96/15 in Turkey in the first photo. In the second, he is accompanied by two other servicemen, *Oblt*. Pommerer (left) and *Kptlt*. Meyer (center). (second photo courtesy of Tobias Weber)

B14. Buddecke (center) and a mechanic pose in front of another E.III in Turkish markings that may have been 108/15.

B16

B15–16. Buddecke and the Halberstadt D.V that he flew toward the end of his time as *Jasta* 4's commanding officer. While describing a November 1916 dogfight in his autobiography (*El Schahin*, p.103), he referred to his unit's planes as "*unsere braunen Ratten*" ("our brown rats"). (B15 is on previous page.)

Halberstadt D.II/III; Halberstadt D.V
(Late August–November 1916)

Buddecke returned to the Western Front to take command of *Jasta* 4 in late August 1916. Numerous photos and other records tell us that the unit was equipped with Halberstadt fighters, beginning with the D.II. We do not know of any photos of Buddecke's early Halberstadt(s), but we do have two snapshots (B15–16) of his later D.V, which would have been from the first batch of 20 ordered in October 1916 (serial numbers 2310–2329/16).[10] He scored no confirmed victories in it, however. *Jasta* 4 eventually traded its Halberstadts for Albatros D.IIs on 27 December 1916 – after Buddecke had left for his second tour in Turkey.

Fokker D.II
(Late August–November 1916)

Thanks to a private album once owned by *Pour le Mérite* recipient Josef Jacobs, we have a picture of Buddecke seated in a Fokker D.II (B17). The man standing near him appears in several other photos in the album, so it is probable that Buddecke was visiting Jacobs' *FFA* 11 or its successor *Jasta* 12, both of which were based at Vaux (near Laon), only about 25 miles south of *Jasta* 4 at Roupy. The D.II might have been a unit "hack" that was primarily used for transportation between German bases.

B17

B17. This photo comes from a private album that once belonged to *Pour le Mérite* ace Josef Jacobs. It shows Buddecke, in the cockpit of a Fokker D.II, in conversation with a man from Jacobs' unit.

B18–19. Buddecke (wearing tropical helmet) shows a Halberstadt D.V to *Gen*. Liman von Sanders (wearing Kalpak cap) sometime during Buddecke's second tour of duty in Turkey in 1917. (first photo courtesy of Tobias Weber)

Halberstadt D.II/III; Halberstadt D.V (Mid-December 1916–January 1918)

Buddecke was back in Turkey in mid-December 1916 and was given the responsibility of defending the western coast of Turkey from Smyrna to Gallipoli. He initially did so with a worn-out airplane though. He complained that his "little biplane really looked pretty sad... Soon after I had gotten it, the tires had gone to the devil; we had installed a thick axle for really heavy aircraft. Then the oppressive heat caused us to use double cooling devices. The wings shook quite alarmingly near the fuselage because the plane had to be left out uncovered in this time of cold nights and rain showers."[11] Buddecke's mention of his "biplane" with "double cooling devices" points us to one of the several Halberstadt D.II/III fighters sent to Turkey in prior months. Some Fokker D-type fighters had also been delivered to Turkey, but they – with their air-cooled rotary engines – did not use radiators. The first of the newer Halberstadt D.V fighters arrived in Turkey in March 1917. Buddecke probably got one of them because he speaks of his "two machine guns" jamming during a fight shortly before 30 March (the Halberstadt D.II/IIIs carried only one gun whereas the D.V carried two in Turkey). If so, it would originally have had one of these serial numbers: 2314/16, 2315/16, 2317/16, 2319/16, 2320/16 or 2324/16.[12] This was probably the plane he flew when he downed two No.2 Wing RNAS aircraft over Smyrna on 30 March 1917 (he again referred to "guns" in his account of the fight). We also have two photos of *Gen*. Liman von Sanders and Buddecke inspecting a Halberstadt D.V (B18–19). Again, we cannot be sure this particular plane was Buddecke's, nor do we know for certain when the photo was taken. A second batch of D.Vs arrived in

December 1917 (shortly before Buddecke's departure from Turkey) and the inspection could have taken place then.

Pfalz D.IIIa 5983/17 (15 February–7 March 1918)

Buddecke was back on the Western Front, serving with *Jasta* 30, on 15 February 1918. B20 is a photo of him in Pfalz D.IIIa 5983/17 during his time with the unit. Given Buddecke's predilection for gambling (according to Erich Serno), the marking on its side could have been a playing card's "spade." He may well have been flying this plane when he brought down his 13th and final victory of the war on 19 February.

Unknown (8–10 March 1918)

Buddecke transferred over to *Jasta* 18 on 8 March to help its commander and his old friend, Rudolf Berthold. The unit was equipped with both Pfalz D.III and Albatros D.V fighters. It is not known which type Buddecke flew on the date of his death, 10 March.

Endnotes
[1] Heinz Nowarra, *50 Jahre Deutsche Luftwaffe I*, p.126, identified the man in front of their plane in B6 as "*Lt. Freiherr* von Marschall." But O'Connor, *Aviation Awards of Imperial Germany 6*, p.175, refers to a "von Marschalk" as having served in *FFA* 23. Thus the photo may be of *Oblt*. Otto *Freiherr* Marschalck von Bachtenbrach who was killed at *AFP* 2's base near Belleglise on 5 January 1916.
[2] See Grosz, *Fokker E.I/II*, p.32. An article in *Die Luftflotte's* June 1917 edition (6, pp.141–42) refers to an *Eindecker* with a damaged wing that had been repaired at a German factory as "*Hauptmann Buddeckes*

B20. Buddecke, in full flight gear, rests atop Pfalz D.IIIa 5983/17 that he evidently flew while serving with *Jasta* 30.

'Laubfrosch.'" (*Hptm*. Buddecke's 'Tree Frog.') The author specifically notes that it was powered by an 80 hp Gnome engine, had wings and an aluminum cowling painted dark green and two seats that the author and a pilot used for a test flight. This then would appear to have been an early, unarmed A.I/M.8 Fokker *Eindecker* (i.e., the 80 hp E.I did not have two seats). Yet Buddecke makes it clear that *FFA* 23's E.I was his first Fokker and never mentions any flight in an A.I/M.8 or anything named 'Laubfrosch.' Even in the event that the author was somehow referring to an E.I, our photos of 15/15 and 36/15 show no evidence of a dark green color scheme. Therefore, the article's representation that Buddecke once flew a green Fokker named 'Tree Frog' must be questioned.

[3] *El Schahin*, p.92.

[4] A photo of it at the school appears in Grosz, *Fokker E.I/II*, p.20.

[5] Allegedly, Fokker E.I 36/15 (werknummer 286) was designated "F 1" in the Turkish army records (see *Over The Front* 11:3, p.258).

[6] *Over The Front* 11:3, p.258.

[7] *El Schahin*, p.68. Allegedly, E.I 36/15 (F 1) had been the first Fokker fighter to arrive in Turkey the previous September, but it was not listed on Buddecke's *Fokkerstaffel* roster in 1916.

[8] *El Schahin*, p.89.

[9] Several differences exist between the E.III seen here and 96/15. E.g., the Turkish insignia on the rudder is smaller, the fuselage insignia's white border is thicker and a compass cage is present in the right wing close to the fuselage. Accordingly, it may have been 108/15, the only other E.III listed with the unit at the time.

[10] See Grosz, *Halberstadt Fighters*, p.46.

[11] *El Schahin*, p.106.

[12] Grosz, *Halberstadt Fighters*, p.47. Grosz lists the Turkish units the planes preliminarily went to, and Turkish *FA* 5 is not among them. Turkish *FA* 6, however, received two (serial numbers 2314/16 and 2319/16). It is quite possible that one was transferred to Buddecke's *FA* 5, which shared in the defense of some of *FA* 6's territory (Dardanelles region).

Hans-Joachim Buddecke (with walking stick) introduces the officers of Turkish *FA* 5 to Archduke Franz Salvator of Austria (marked with 'x') while the unit's ground personnel look on. (photo courtesy of Tobias Weber)

Turkish *FA* 5's aircraft lined up on Galata airfield in October 1917. They were awaiting inspection by Kaiser Wilhelm II who, according to Buddecke's note on the photo's back, never showed up. (photo courtesy of Tobias Weber)

Buddecke – Military Service

Significant Dates

22 Aug 1890	born in Berlin
spring 1904	entered Cadet Corps
1910	certified as a *Leutnant*
1913	traveled to the United States
spring 1914	taught himself to fly in Chicago
Aug 1914	returned to Germany
2 Sep 1914	assigned to *Flieger-Ersatz-Abteilung* at Darmstadt
27 Sep 1914	assigned to *Flieger-Ersatz-Abteilung* 3
20 Oct 1914	assigned to *Ettapen-Flugzeug-Park* 2
12 Jan 1915	assigned to *Feldflieger-Abteilung* 27
10 Jun 1915	assigned to *Feldflieger-Abteilung* 23
late Aug 1915	first flight in Fokker *Eindecker*
19 Sep 1915	first victory
Dec 1915	joined German Military Mission in Turkey
Jan 1916	assigned to Turkish *Flieger-Abteilung* 6
14 Apr 1916	awarded *Pour le Mérite*
25 Aug 1916	assigned to *Jasta* 4
mid-Dec 1916	returned to Turkey; assigned to Turkish *Flieger-Abteilung* 5
15 Feb 1918	assigned to *Jasta* 30
19 Feb 1918	final victory (#13)
8 Mar 1918	assigned to *Jasta* 18
10 Mar 1918	killed in action
22 Mar 1918	buried in Berlin

Service Units

1910–1913	*Leibgarde-Infanterie-Regiment (1. Grossherzoglich Hessisches)* Nr. 115.
2–26 Sep 1914	*Flieger-Ersatz-Abteilung* ?
27 Sep–19 Oct 1914	*Flieger-Ersatz-Abteilung* 3
20 Oct 1914–11 Jan 1915	*Ettapen-Flugzeug-Park* 2
12 Jan–9 Jun 1915	*Feldflieger-Abteilung* 27
10 Jun–Nov 1915	*Feldflieger-Abteilung* 23
Jan–early Aug 1916	Turkish *Flieger-Abteilung* 6
25 Aug–Nov 1916	*Jagdstaffel* 4
mid-Dec 1916–Jan 1918	Turkish *Flieger-Abteilung* 5
15 Feb–7 Mar 1918	*Jagdstaffel* 30
8–10 Mar 1918	*Jagdstaffel* 18

Awards

early 1915	Pilot's Badge – Germany
Jan–Jul 1915	Iron Cross, 2nd Class – Prussia*
Jan–Jul 1915	Military Merit Order, 4th Class with Swords – Bavaria*
16 Oct 1915	Military St. Henry Order, Knight – Saxony
23 Oct 1915	War Merit Cross, 2nd Class – Brunswick
late Dec 1915/ Jan 1916	Pilot's Badge – Ottoman Empire**
late Jan/early Feb 1916	Liakat Medal in Gold and in Silver – Ottoman Empire
18 Feb 1916	Royal Hohenzollern House Order, Knight's Cross with Swords – Prussia***
14 Apr 1916	*Pour le Mérite* – Prussia
Jun/Jul 1916	Imtiaz Medal in Gold and in Silver – Ottoman Empire
unknown	Iron Cross, 1st Class – Prussia (possibly after 1st victory, 19 Sep 1915)
unknown	*Ehrenbecher* – Germany (possibly 25 Dec 1915)****
unknown	War Medal – Ottoman Empire (probably with Liakat Medal in late Jan/early Feb 1916)
unknown	Field Pilot's Badge, Army – Austria-Hungary

*wearing ribbon in photo with *FFA* 27

**probably upon entering German Military Mission in Turkey. Photos show that it was of a special design: wings ran from 2 o'clock to 8 o'clock position vs standard badge's 10 o'clock to 4 o'clock.

***date of congratulatory telegram provided by Tobias Weber

****Boelcke (6 vics), Immelmann (7 vics) retrospectively received theirs this date; Buddecke had 3 vics

Buddecke – Victory List

No.	Date	Aircraft	Location, Unit & Crew*
1	19 Sep 1915	BE.2c 2008	near Saint-Quentin – RFC 8: 2Lt. WH Nixon (KIA), Cpt. JNS Stott (WIA/POW)
2	23 Oct	BE.2c 2017	near Saint-Quentin – RFC 13: Cpt. CH Marks, 2Lt. WG Lawrence (b-KIA)
3	11 Nov	BE.2c 1725	near Saint-Quentin – RFC 8: Lt. WA Harvey (WIA/POW)
4	6 Jan 1916	Farman	between Özbek and Karacaören – Esc MF98.T: B de Conte (KIA)
5	12 Jan	Farman	near Seddülbahir – No.2/3 Wing RNAS: FltSubLt. JS Bolas (KIA), Midsh. DM Branson (WIA/POW)
6	25 Jan	?	Dardanelles region – ?
7	27 Jan	?	Dardanelles region – ?
8	16 Sep	?	near Chaulnes
9	22 Sep	FE.2b 4937 OR FE.2b 6937	near Combles – RFC 18: 2Lt. F Hall (DOW), Lt. BF Randall OR near Nesle – RFC 18: Sgt. T Jones (DOW), 2Lt. FAA Hewson (WIA/POW)
10	23 Sep	BE.12 6167	near Sailly – RFC 21: Lt. JMJ Kenny (POW/DOW)
11	30 Mar 1917	Henri Farman F27 N3024	Izmir – No.2 Wing RNAS: FltSubLt. BA Trechmann, LdMidSh. WA Jones (b-POW)
12	30 Mar 1917	Nieu. 12 9203	Izmir – No.2 Wing RNAS: FltLt. JE Morgan, FltSubLt. A Sandell (b-KIA)
13	19 Feb 1918	Sopwith Camel B9185 OR B9171	near Neuve-Chapelle – RFC 80: 2Lt. SR Pinder (KIA) or 2Lt. E Westmoreland (KIA)

*pilot listed first

b-	both occupants	KIA	killed in action
DOW	died of wounds	POW	prisoner of war

The ground personnel of Turkish *FA* 5. (photo courtesy of Tobias Weber)

Kurt Wintgens

Above: A pleasing portrait of *Lt.* Kurt Wintgens wearing his *Pour le Mérite* and displaying ribbons for four of his other decorations: Royal Hohenzollern House Order, Knight's Cross with Swords; Iron Cross, 2nd Class; Military Merit Order, 4th Class with Swords; Albert Order, Knight 2nd Class with Swords. It was taken at Karl Zinne's studio in Minden while Wintgens was home on leave in August 1916.

Wintgens – The Man

Youth and Early Career

Kurt Wintgens was born on 1 August 1894 in the northern Bavarian town of Bad Neustadt an der Saale. His father, an *Oberstleutnant* (lieutenant colonel) in the military, soon moved the family – which also consisted of mother Martha (née Bohlmann), brother Max and sister

Anneliese – further north to Minden.[1] He was quite mechanically inclined and as a young man, joined the region's Aviation Association where he and his close friend, Karl Wömper, built flying model airplanes. Wintgens passed his high school final examination on his 18th birthday and enlisted with *Telegraphen-Bataillon* Nr.2 (a wireless unit) in Frankfurt/Oder as a *Fahnenjunker* (ensign) early the next year. He evidently excelled in his early military career because he was appointed to the prestigious War Academy in Bad Hersfeld, where he was studying when 1914's "Guns of August" heralded the onset of the first global war.

By his own account, Wintgens (now a *Leutnant*) initially served as a *Fliegertruppe* (Air Service) observer in August and September 1914; but then he was recalled to his old *Telegraphen-Bataillon* due to a shortage of officers. He was with that unit when it entered Poland as part of *Armee-Oberkommando* 9 and remained attached to it until February 1915. Though he is said to have won the Iron Cross, 2nd Class for his bravery in Poland, Wintgens himself did not seem overly impressed with his accomplishments when he self-deprecatingly wrote his friend Wömper: "My glorious business there has been described in a long article titled 'Wireless Troops Under Fire!' in several big German papers on their honor page. Minden, which is mentioned as my hometown in that article, simply has to build me a triumphal arch when next time I circle proudly over the town!"[2]

Right: This portrait of Kurt Wintgens, published in a German newspaper, was taken by O. Heinrich in Frankfurt/Oder when Wintgens was a *Fahnenjunker* with *Telegraphen-Bataillon* Nr.2.

Airman

Obviously not pleased with wireless troop duties, Wintgens told Wömper that "I blackmailed myself to *Flieger-Bataillon* 1 for pilot's training." When advising his friend on how to join the *Fliegertruppe*, Wintgens elaborated further: "First, you have to write a request containing that you have busied

yourself with the technical aspects of flight for such a time, constructed, flown yourself, are well-versed in the theoretical and practical side of the business... You would have joined the *Fliegertruppe* but for domestic circumstances, etc., etc., etc. Easily lie until you're black in the face! Later, nobody asks any questions. You should have seen my request!" After a month or so with *Flieger-Bataillon* 1 at Döberitz, Wintgens continued his flight training at Anthony Fokker's factory at Schwerin-Görries. It appears that a prior connection with Fokker played a part in that transfer, because when speaking of it Wintgens referred to his having had "enormous luck" in meeting up with his "old acquaintance, Fokker."

Wintgens trained in several early Fokker designs including the M.5L monoplane and M.7 and M.10 biplanes. His teachers were "some old Kanonen, as for instance Scherff, the well-known flier with the Turks, and Schmidt, who formerly flew Dornier and then Torpedo-Kühlstein monoplanes."[3] His first solo flights occurred in April and during one of them the engine malfunctioned in his Fokker monoplane. Wintgens, just 150 meters above the Bay of Lübeck, had little choice but to put the nose down and hope for the best. He barely made it to the coast, skimming across the water with only one or two meters to spare before he crash landed – fortunately without injury. By early May, he had passed two of the three flight examinations required for his pilot's license. Then he was transferred back to Döberitz where he successfully performed his final test.

Back in March, a pre-war French aviator named Roland Garros had mounted a forward-facing machine gun on the nose of his Morane Saulnier monoplane. To protect his propeller, he had attached metal plates to each blade to deflect any bullets that

Above: *Lt.* Kurt Wintgens poses alongside his "old acquaintance" Anthony Fokker in August 1916. This photo later appeared on postcard number 400 of the famous Sanke series.

Right: Judging by the Fokker M-type biplane fuselage in the background at right and the presence of several civilians, this photograph of Kurt Wintgens behind the wheel of a car may have been taken during his training period at Fokker's military flight school.

struck them while firing the gun. Garros shot down several surprised Germans before he himself was forced to land behind enemy lines on 19 April and his apparatus was unveiled to the German military. In a 13 May letter to his friend Wömper, Wintgens prophetically mused: "In the field I'd like to fly the smallest and fastest Fokker-type with the Garros installation, which enables a built-in machine gun to fire through the propeller. You have to aim the whole of the machine which must be easy with the enormous sensitivity of the machine. Then I, as a single-seater, would take on every biplane, which I can clearly outclimb and attack from above and behind." Just three days later, a German aviation official reported to his superiors that "interesting firing trials from a monoplane (through the propeller, a French invention, that became known on the occasion of Garros' capture) will take place (at Döberitz) on Wednesday, 19 May at noon, or Thursday, 20 May in the morning."[4] Wintgens was probably in attendance, watching as his dream began to take a palpable form.

Fighter Pilot

Anthony Fokker did one better than Garros and developed an interruptor gear mechanism that prevented his forward-facing machine gun from firing whenever a propeller blade came before its muzzle. After successfully mounting the synchronization mechanism on his Fokker 80 hp M.5K scout, the military placed an order for a new armed fighter type, subsequently designated as the Fokker E.I. The first seven E.Is were delivered to the Front in June 1916 even as Fokker was demonstrating and seeking approval of his more powerful 100 hp E.II fighter.[5] E.I 1/15 went to *Lt.* Otto Parschau, 3/15 to *Lt.* Oswald Boelcke, and 5/15 to Wintgens – no doubt because of his close ties to Fokker. Wintgens tested the plane in Mannheim and was supposed to take it to *Feldflieger-Abteilung (FFA)* 48 (part of *Armee-Abteilung* Gaede) near Mühlhausen when he was diverted to another hot spot on the Front "where lately a Parasol fighter-monoplane à la Garros has made its presence felt." He flew to Bavarian *FFA* 6b's base outside of Sarrebourg-Buhl (via Strasbourg) in late June and began his patrols. On 2 July, Wintgens reported: "I had flown to the Front a couple of times without seeing an opponent, until yesterday evening when the big moment came. Time: 6 o'clock. Place: east of Lunéville. Altitude: between 2000 and 2500 meters. Suddenly I noticed a monoplane in front of me, about 35 meters higher. At the same moment he dived on me, firing his machine gun fiercely and decently. He missed wildly though since I dived at

Above: Supreme Headquarters recalled the following in its obituary for Kurt Wintgens: "He was very talented musically... The accordion was his indispensable travel kit; whenever he visited, he would bring it with him and spread cheer all around." (*Flugsport 21*, p.563) This is a snapshot of him and his accordion when he was at *FFA* 6b.

once in an opposite direction under him. After four attacks I reached his altitude in a large turn, and now my machine gun did some talking as well. I attacked at such a close distance that we looked each other in the face. After my third attack, he did the most stupid thing that he could do – he fled. I turned the crate on the spot and had him immediately, beautifully, in my sight. Rapid fire for about four seconds, and down went his nose. I could follow him until 500 meters, then, unfortunately, I was fired upon too hotly from the ground, the fight being far over the French lines. Hopefully, I'll soon meet a biplane." French documents stated that a Morane L Parasol from *Escadrille (Esc.)* MS48, after engaging a Fokker over Forêt Domaniale de Parroy, was forced to land east of Lunéville around 6:00 pm, and that both occupants, *Capitaine* Paul du Peuty (pilot) and *Sous-Lieutenant* Louis de Boutiny (observer) were wounded.[6] Wintgens was not credited with an official victory, however, most likely because the plane landed safely behind its own lines. Still, this action is now recognized as the first time the Fokker *Eindecker* was used to force down an enemy plane.

On 12 July, Wintgens reported more action: "Many interesting things have happened here since the last time [I wrote]. I have appeared twice in the German general staff announcements – first, forcing a French machine to make a hurried landing and then successfully defending against three enemy fighting machines... the latter business was not easy though. The scrap started with a Parasol, and in the heat of battle I followed him over the airfield at Lunéville, where two others – another Parasol and a Voisin – greeted me with cordial machine gun fire. The fight was on for 1½ hours, then all were gone and I could proudly leave the spot with 12 liters of fuel left and in complete darkness. My machine, however, looked pretty beaten up. Propeller grazed, causing trouble to the engine. Machine gun defect and elevator hit... The day before yesterday we offered the people of Lunéville a real air battle in which ten to twelve machines took part. The competitors got a belly-full. It was a view which I will not forget for the rest of my life. It must have been a wonderful sight, especially from the ground. In the evening sky the fighting mono- and biplanes, all of them firing machine guns, and in between the bursting shells of the antiaircraft guns. You might get pretty jumpy in such a fight. Thank God I have no nerves." Historian Reinhard Kastner discovered a document in Bavaria's Stadtarchiv that describes the latter fight.[7] Issued from "Bühl-Saarburg" (now Sarrebourg-Buhl) by *FFA* 6b (part of *Armee-Abteilung* Falkenhausen), the report states that at around 7:20 in the evening four of their aircraft engaged enemy planes that had crossed the lines running from Dombasle-sur-Meurthe to Saint-Clément in the vicinity of Lunéville, and that a "very lively, proper air battle ensued." The report similarly mentioned the many biplanes, a French monoplane, the close in-fighting and antiaircraft fire (even though the planes were at times only 100 meters apart). A surprising revelation is that Wintgens was not flying his *Eindecker* during the battle; rather, the document – written by the unit's CO who was also in the fight – states that Wintgens was manning the machine gun of Aviatik C.181, piloted by a *Lt*. Schinnerer.[8] It would have been very interesting indeed if Wintgens had been able to shoot down one of his opponents from the back seat of the Aviatik.

In the same letter, Wintgens noted that he was being sent to *FFA* 48 near Mühlhausen where a French monoplane airman "has decently cleaned things up."[9] He also said that he did not belong to any one *Flieger-Abteilung* "but am independent."

Thus early in his career and before the advent of the *Kampfeinsitzer-Kommando* (single-seater fighter command) units that would be formed in 1916, Wintgens had a roving commission and was sent to trouble spots along the Lorraine Front as needed.

Shortly after his arrival at *FFA* 48, Wintgens was granted his first official victory on 15 July. The airplane reportedly fell in the Vosges region near the Col de la Schlucht, but there are no French or British candidates that suit such an identification. Still, bearing in mind that the German criteria for allowing a victory claim were particularly strict at the time and that several of Wintgens' other claims had been disallowed, today's historians generally accept this one and have assigned the first official victory in a Fokker *Eindecker* to Wintgens.[10]

Wintgens was then credited with a second success that was either a reconsideration of his 1 July fight or another now unknown event. On 12 August, he informed Wömper of his third that came down on 9 August: "It was a very interesting and exciting fight which ended with a 'little' explosion of the French battle biplane... The fellow almost took me with him when he went down in flames from 2700 meters, for the last 50 rounds I fired at him were from a distance of only two aeroplane lengths. But I saved the situation via an involuntary looping. It really was wonderful; due to my superior speed and maneuverability I could continuously maintain my position in his machine gun's blind spot." His victims were *Maréchal-des-Logis* Onèsime Louis Paul Victor (pilot) and *Sergent* Phillipe Marius Toureille, flying in an *Esc.* VB112 Voisin that crashed near Gondrexange. Certain evidence suggests that Wintgens may have been with *FFA* 67 for this engagement. *FFA* 67, created on 30 June 1915, was located at Bathelémont-lès-Bauzemont in September 1915 and then moved to Lorquin for the remainder of the year.[11] Lorquin, only 8 kilometers southwest of Sarrebourg, was called "Lörchingen" by the Germans. When Wintgens specifically mentioned that he was with *Feldflieger-Abteilung* 6b in his letter of 2 July 1915, he used the return address "Bühl-Saarburg" (an airfield still exists at present-day Sarrebourg-Buhl 2½ kilometers southeast of Sarrebourg). In his letters dated 14 August and 20 October, he used only "Saarburg." *Lt*. Georg Rockenhäuser and *Lt*. Willi Maguhn of *FFA* 67 were listed in German records as having been killed on 1 January 1916 at "Saarburg, Lörchingen" (i.e., Sarrebourg, Lorquin).[12] Thus it is possible that "Saarburg," as opposed to *FFA* 6b's "Bühl-Saarburg," was the general address Wintgens used when he was with *FFA* 67. Having made no prior direct reference to *FFA* 67 in his letters, this would

Above: Kurt Wintgens poses for the camera wearing his parade dress belt and officer's sword knot (dangling underneath his tunic). The absence of any sign of his Royal Hohenzollern House Order, Knight 2nd Class with Swords, points to this picture being taken prior to its award in late June 1916 – perhaps when Wintgens was home on leave in September 1915.

explain the endnote to his letter of 12 January 1916: "I hope to be going back to *Abteilung* 67 again, very soon."

Returning to Wintgens' 12 August letter, he disclosed: "Shortly I'll get a small monoplane with a 160 hp (!) Gnôme." This early reference to the Fokker E.IV is another clear indication of Wintgens' close relationship with Anthony Fokker. The E.IV was still under development in August 1915 and the first of its type, E.IV 122/15, was not accepted until 19 September.[13] Wintgens had to wait longer than he thought, however, because E.IV 122/15 went to *Lt.* Otto Parschau and the next one, 123/15, was taken by *Lt.* Oswald Boelcke in December. Wintgens finally received his E.IV 124/15 in January 1916 – one

of three delivered to the Front that month.

Wintgens was unable to gain any more confirmed victories during this waiting period due to a decided lack of air activity, though he did mention several interesting experiences. For example, he experimented with throwing bombs at the enemy from his monoplane, embarked on a high altitude flight that left him dizzy from lack of oxygen, and participated in the interrogation of a captured Morane Saulnier pilot. Regarding the air war itself he wrote: "...all is as normal as possible," "not much news here...," "nothing special has happened here lately" and "...everything has been very quiet." The few fights that he was able to scrape up ended with frustrating gun stoppages. It also appears that he was still moving about from one unit to another. If our theory above about the differentiaton between "Bühl-Saarburg" and "Saarburg" addresses is correct, then he went from *FFA* 67 to *FFA* 6b in September and back again to *FFA* 67 in October. But his precise whereabouts for the remainder of 1915 are unknown.

Things changed after his Christmas leave to Minden, when in early January 1916 he encountered and "shot down a Farman two-seater after a short air battle. The aeroplane was directing artillery fire, and was doing a bad job of paying attention to what was going on around it... I put 200 bullet holes into the machine's body, without incurring a single shot myself. All during this time he was doing all sorts of aerobatics. With the earth coming rapidly nearer, at a height of 600 meters, I was hit by a particularly good shot from the French trenches and could see the sun shining through my plane. But everything turned out well..." Though the victory went unconfirmed, Wintgens was apparently consoled by his recent gift of "a very beautiful, silver honor goblet that I can take home with me"– that is, the *Ehrenbecher* that was just beginning to be issued to airmen who had already achieved air victories and henceforth would be awarded upon the occasion of an airman's first victory.[14]

Wintgens was now serving with *FFA* 12 at Burlingshofen (Burlioncourt), according to the return address on his letter of 12 January 1916.[15] We have further confirmation of his presence there by virtue of several photographs of him together with Walter Höhndorf, who is said to have served with *FFA* 12 and *FFA* 67 before moving on to *KEK* Vaux. One of them shows both men next to Höhndorf's first victory of 17 January 1916 whose nose had been overpainted with the phrase: "*Erbeutet im Luftkampf von Feldflieger* 12" ("Captured in air combat with *Feldflieger-Abteilung* 12").[16] After January, however, it is difficult to pinpoint precisely what units Wintgens served in and when, because

Above: *Lt*. Walter Höhndorf stands in the cockpit of the Voisin from VB105 he vanquished on 17 January 1916. Kurt Wintgens is on the ground, second from left.

his letters no longer bore specific return addresses. Given what appears to have been his possible migratory history from unit to unit, no wonder he apologized to Wömper in his next letter dated 25 January: "I am very sorry for not having been able to fulfill my idea of visiting you in Freiburg. It was not possible, partly due to my continuous postings, however much I wanted to."

On 24 January, Wintgens encountered a Caudron: "I met my old opponent, the twin-engined large machine with which I had had quite a run of combats that had all ended without a decision due to a lot of various reasons. This time, however, engine and machine gun worked perfectly. The two of us were about 3600 meters up and I attacked him from the left in such a manner that he could only use one machine gun. At a distance of about 80 meters I started to fire continuously and apparently hit the pilot well, for suddenly the machine turned on its left wing, came straight at me so that I could only just evade him, and then he fell down vertically when about 20 meters away from me. Not lazy at that, I went after him like lightning. After 400 meters he flattened out again and received another burst from me whereupon, suddenly, a colossal smoke cloud came from his right engine. When by chance I looked back, I noticed that because of a very strong eastern wind, I had been driven far over

the lines, so that I had to leave him to his fate. I take it that he met the earth fast. Back home I saw that he had hit me with a bullet through the right forerib, but it had all held together well until I got down." Once again, Wintgens was able to chalk up only another unconfirmed claim because it fell well behind its own lines.

Wintgens contracted a case of influenza in the first week of February and was sent to nearby Strasbourg to recuperate. While there, he wrote that he was anxious "to hurry back to the Front where my new aeroplane and I are needed very badly. Most of the machines have a bad rate of climb and are very clumsy... They do not know what they are in for!" He now had his 160 hp Fokker E.IV and was obviously looking forward to using it.

Despite his eagerness, several months passed before he was able to achieve his next successes – which then fell in rapid succession on 20 and 21 May 1916. Wintgens reported: "My fourth was a 'Nieuport *avion de chasse*' of the latest type and with a new marking on the upper wing (not the usual cockades). At first I thought I had an Englishman before me and attacked with doubled fury... The machine had 80–100 hits and partly looked like a porcupine. The observer was riddled indeed, the pilot had the good fortune to emerge without heavy wounds, in spite of

Ein am 20. 5. 16 in Wich abgestürztes franz. Flugzeug

Above and Left: Two views of the Nieuport XII from *Escadrille* N68 that Wintgens shot down on 20 May 1916 for his fourth official victory. As he stated in one of his letters, it carried new markings on the upper wings (four vertical columns made up of filled circles) instead of the usual French cockade.

being hit five times; one of these under the left eye – the bullet exited at the right eye. I had an interesting discussion with him in the hospital." The unfortunate pilot was *Maréchal-des-Logis* Leon Cesar Léon Beauchamps and the even less fortunate observer was *Sous-Lieutenant* Debacker, both from *Esc.* N68. Wintgens forced their Nieuport XII down near Château-Salins and one surviving photo (above) attests to its unusual markings. "My fifth, the next day, was a twin-engined Caudron. Two Le Rhône engines, two tractor propellers, tailbooms, four rudders, about 20 meter broad wings – quite a fellow! From 4000 meters he went down vertically. After the 'landing' the engines were 1½ meters in the earth. The crate had automatically disintegrated and was spread out over several square kilometers. Yesterday the crew was buried with military honors; they had fought gamely to the end." Details concerning this plane and crew are presently unknown.

Wintgens' next victim, a Farman from MF70 manned by *Lieutenant* Brunel and *Sous-Lieutenant* Pierre Hemand, fell to earth near Bezange-la-Grande on 17 June. Wintgens wrote: "It was a wonderful fight. He exploded marvellously. He was already behind the French lines when the pilot, who hung dead over the right side, apparently touched a rudder in some way. The machine turned and fell burning into the German lines, greeted by a thunderous hurrah from the whole of the Front." As a result of this sixth official victory, Wintgens was awarded the Royal Hohenzollern House Order, Knight's Cross with Swords sometime in late June before it was announced in the 1 July 1916 edition of *Militär Wochenblatt*.

Wintgens mentioned that during the same fight on 17 June, just one hundred meters away, Walter Höhndorf "fought a Nieuport" – a clear indication that they were serving together in the same unit. Photographic evidence informs us that they were still together after Wintgens' receipt of the Royal Hohenzollern House Order up though his *Pour le Mérite* award on 1 July 1916 (see below). On 19 July 1916, Saxony decorated Wintgens with its Albert Order, Knight 2nd Class with Swords in recognition

Above: Wintgens (third from right) sits down to a meal, joined by his comrade *Lt.* Walter Höhndorf (second from left). Wintgens is wearing his Royal Hohenzollern House Order, Knight 2nd Class with Swords, in his tunic's second buttonhole – usually a sign that it had been recently awarded. Wintgens' Hohenzollern House Order came to him sometime in late June shortly before his *Pour le Mérite* on 1 July 1916. He is not wearing that decoration, however, so the photo originated between those two events.

of his performance with *FFA* 67. Though this could have been for his stints with the unit in the last half of 1915, it might also be an indication that Wintgens and Höhndorf – who is often reported to have served with *FFA* 67 after *FFA* 12 – were both members of *FFA* 67 around this time. On the other hand, Walter Höhndorf's 10 April 1916 victory is said to have occurred while he was serving with *Fokkerstaffel* Falkenhausen – a unit formed on 9 February 1916 that worked alongside *FFA* 67 within *Generaloberst* Ludwig von Falkenhausen's *Armee* Falkenhausen. The fact that Wintgens' later 1 July *Pour le Mérite* award was celebrated in a photograph taken with the general indicates that Wintgens and Höhndorf may have been serving with *Fokkerstaffel* Falkenhausen for some time (see p.46 below).

On the afternoon of 23 June, *Sergent* Victor Chapman of N124 (Lafayette *Escadrille*) was engaged by three German fighters and shot down in Nieuport XVI 1334 near Haumont-prés-Samogneux. Though

several historians have attributed his demise to Kurt Wintgens, several factors do not support such a claim. First, the 24 June *Bericht der Oberste Heeresleitung* for the prior day's events made a clear distinction between Chapman's action and Wintgens': "A French monoplane fighter [SIC] was brought down in air combat near Haumont; *Lt.* Wintgens shot down his seventh enemy airplane, a French biplane, near Blâmont." Second, Blâmont is well within the range of Wintgens' usual hunting grounds in the Lorraine region whereas Haumont-prés-Samogneux (where Chapman crashed) is considerably farther northwest above Verdun[17]. Norman Franks tells us that a Farman flown by pilot *Adjutant* Jacques Semelin and *Sous-Lieutenant* Gallon of MF58 fell near Blâmont that day, but that it may actually have collided with a Fokker flown by *Gefr.* Hermann Keller of *FFA* 32.[18] According to the unit's war diary, however, Keller was killed that day at Bertincourt – which is nowhere near Blâmont –

Above: Wintgens, with his glasses in his left hand, rests on the remains of what probably was his eighth victim. Various factors (the airplane fell behind enemy lines, was captured intact, burned, disintegrated in midair, does not match other photographs) disqualify his first seven victories. This leaves us with his eighth because he is not wearing his *Pour le Mérite* here, which he did thereafter.

Above: This is a group portrait of some of the men who attended Kurt Wintgens' *Pour le Mérite* investiture ceremony sometime after its official award date of 1 July 1916. *Generaloberst* Ludwig von Falkenhausen, in charge of the German 6th Army's *Armee-Abteilung* Falkenhausen, stands at center. Wintgens and Walter Höhndorf are to the right and left, respectively, of Falkenhausen in the front row and Walter Kypke, a future ace, is second from the left. Wintgens, Höhndorf, Falkenhausen, the officer at far left and the one between Wintgens and Falkenhausen also posed together in a picture in front of Wintgens' Halberstadt D.II that was taken sometime before the ceremony (see p.68).

Von der Feier einer Fliegerabteilung im Westen bei Verleihung des Ordens Pour le Mérite.

Above: A photograph of personnel from *Feldflieger-Abteilung* 23 and its *KEK* Vaux detachment. Though various versions have been published in several other works, this is how it appeared in a wartime German newspaper that identified it as a "celebration of the conferment of the *Pour le Mérite* order at a *Flieger-Abteilung* on the West Front." (*Illustrierte Geschichte des Weltkrieges 5*, p.340) Of the three men sitting in the foreground wearing that decoration, the most recent recipients were *Oblt*. Ernst von Althaus (right) who was granted his award on 21 July, and *Lt*. Walter Höhndorf (left), who got his the day before on 20 July. Kurt Wintgens, sitting between them, had received his weeks earlier on 1 July. Thus this probably was a joint celebration held in honor of Höhndorf and Althaus. Some believe this picture is evidence that Kurt Wintgens served in *KEK* Vaux whereas others think that he was just visiting from nearby *KEK* Bertincourt as as a close friend of Höhndorf's and another knight of the *Orden Pour le Mérite*. Other identifiable men: *Hptm*. Hermann Palmer, CO of *FFA* 23 (second row, center, in white tunic), *Oblt*. Rudolf Berthold (second row, far right), *Vzfw*. Josef Veltjens (back row, second from left), Lt. Walter Gnamm (back row, sixth from left), *Lt*. Wilhelm Frankl (back row, second from right), *Lt*. Alfred Lenz (back row, far right).

while testing a Rumpler. Therefore, MF58's Farman is the best candidate for Wintgens' seventh victory. Whoever it was, we at least know he was not flying his usual E.IV mount that day. On 22 June, Wintgens wrote: "This afternoon my 160 hp engine goes to Oberursel. Yesterday it collected a bullet in a too strenuous chase of a Farman..."

Wintgens shot down his all-important eighth, a Farman that crashed southwest of Château-Salins, on 30 June.[19] At the time, an airman had to have eight victories in order to qualify for the *Pour le Mérite* and Wintgens was duly awarded his on 1 July. Photographic evidence suggests that he was decorated in the field by no less a personage than

Above: On 21 July 1916, 2Lt. R.M. Wilson-Browne of RFC No.12 Squadron had to leave his observer behind in order to compensate for the weight of the bomb he was supposed to drop on the railway bridge at Aubigny-au-Bac. Along the way, he ran into Fokker fighters flown by Kurt Wintgens and *Lt.* Albert Oesterreicher. Wilson-Browne was severely wounded during the ensuing fight and crash-landed his BE.2c 2100 aircraft near the town. Here we see the plane and Wilson-Browne after he had been dragged unconscious from it. He was taken prisoner but succumbed to his wounds later the same day.

Generaloberst Ludwig von Falkenhausen, the head of one of the army groups within which Wintgens operated. It also indicates that he gained this victory in a recently-arrived Halberstadt D.II.

Soon after this, Wintgens was transferred to a *Kampfeinsitzer-Kommando (KEK)* unit – either *KEK* Bertincourt (also called *KEK Nord*) or *KEK Vaux* (also called *KEK Süd*).[20] Both operated in the same vicinity and their men were often photographed together, so once again it is difficult to say precisely where Wintgens was stationed and when. Though the majority of historians seem to think he went to *KEK* Vaux, a few have offered that Wintgens' service record indicates that he joined the German 1st Army's efforts on the Somme in the summer of 1916. On 19 July 1916, part of the 2nd Army was split off to create the 1st Army. Wintgens' 9th, 10th and 11th victories fell either within the 1st Army's territory (Arras, Achiet-le-Petit) or just outside it in the neighboring 6th Army's territory (Aubigny-au-Bac). Thus it is argued that Wintgens probably belonged to a *KEK* operating with the 1st

Army (as *KEK* Bertincourt did) rather than *KEK* Vaux, which was with the 2nd Army. Additionally, *KEK* Bertincourt was at the core of the formation of *Jasta* 1, a unit we know Wintgens later joined. Yet a recently-discovered photo set, recorded together on the same postcard-sized print, points back to *KEK* Vaux. One of the images (see p.65 below) shows Wintgens' Fokker E.IV 124/15 decorated with a wreath encircling the number "12." The other (see below) has Wintgens in conversation with a captured British pilot in a *KEK* Vaux automobile in front of Château Vaux. Assuming that the pilot was 2Lt. L.N. Graham, the man Wintgens counted as his 12th on 30 July, we have additional evidence that Wintgens was with *KEK* Vaux at the time. As we are about to see, evidence also exists that Wintgens may have been assigned to *Jasta* 4 before going to *Jasta* 1. And what was the unit from which *Jasta* 4 emerged? *KEK* Vaux.

Whether he was with *KEK* Vaux or *KEK* Bertincourt, Wintgens was clearly in the thick of things over the Somme and added four more aircraft

Above: Wintgens' 12th victim, Martinsyde G100 7471 of RFC No.27 Squadron, was forced down near Péronne on 30 July 1916. Here we see it under guard after its wounded pilot, 2Lt. L.N Graham, had been taken away for treatment as a prisoner-of-war.

to his tally in July (including his first double victory on 21 July). Another came on 2 August, but then his guns fell uncharacteristically silent until the following mid-September. This was because he was back in Germany in August, visiting his home in Minden.[21]

According to *Jasta* 1's *Kriegstagebuch* (war diary), Kurt Wintgens and Walter Höhndorf were both in its original complement when it was formed on 22 August 1916.[22] Yet Hans-Joachim Buddecke stated in his autobiography that after he became the *Staffelführer* (commanding officer) of *Jasta* 4, "when we set up our tents again at Vaux in order to put over a dozen airplanes inside them, I counted five gentlemen with the *Pour le Mérite*... Wintgens and Höhndorf, as was their habit, flew together."[23] We also have a photo of Höhndorf atop his Halberstadt fighter reporting something to Wintgens, *Oblt.* Hans-Joachin Buddecke and *Hptm.* Hermann Palmer, CO of *FFA* 23 that was stationed at Roupy and used to be the "parent" of

KEK Vaux. Perhaps Wintgens and Höhndorf – like Leopold Reimann, another of *Jasta* 1's original members – were transferred out of *Jasta* 1 soon after *Jasta* 4's formation on 25 August.[24] If so, neither of them was credited with a victory while there. When they did score again in mid-September, they were back at *Jasta* 1.

Wintgens achieved his second double victory on 14 September: a Nieuport near Bussu in the morning and a "pusher type" early in the evening north of Rancourt. No likely candidate for the Nieuport victory has been discovered to date; but there are two possibilities for the evening victory

Above: This snapshot was placed above another depicting Wintgens' Fokker E.IV 124/15 marked in celebration of his 12th victory, which suggests that the captured British pilot seen here was 2Lt. L.N. Graham of RFC No.27 Squadron who was brought down in Martinsyde G100 7471 on 30 July near Péronne. Wintgens is conversing with the pilot (see blowup at left) in the back seat of an automobile whose nose is marked with "*FeldFlieg. Abt. 23, Kampf-Einsitzer-Kaffel.*" – a reference to *KEK* Vaux of *FFA* 23. Was "*Kaffel*" a shortened form of "*Kampfstaffel*" similar to *Kasta*?

Left: Wintgens' final victory, Martinsyde G100 7498 of RFC No.27 Squadron, in custody at a German airfield. He had forced it down on 24 September near Ribécourt-la-Tour, where its pilot, 2Lt. E.N. Wingfield, was taken prisoner.

Right: One of several photos that seem to support Hans-Joachim Buddecke's statement that Wintgens and Höhndorf served with his *Jasta* 4 during its early days. From left to right, Buddecke, Wintgens, and *Hptm*. Hermann Palmer (CO of *FFA* 23, also stationed near Vaux) listen as Höhndorf speaks from atop a Halberstadt fighter.

Above & Right: In the first image, Wintgens' coffin, flanked by an honor guard and surrounded by wreaths and garlands, lies in state in a "little evangelical church" in Saint-Quentin. The *Ordenskissen* (awards cushion) to which his decorations were pinned for display rests at the head of the coffin. The second picture is a closeup of that *Ordenskissen*. When examined under magnification, Wintgens' *Pour le Mérite* (at top) shows signs of damage – arms bent and enamel broken away at the center. Several photos demonstrate that Wintgens wore his *Pour le Mérite* into combat, so the damage seen here probably occurred as a result of his crash.

Facing page: Wintgens' casket, draped in black and white, rests on a motorized transport with an honor guard. Two wreaths, made in the form of a *Pour le Mérite*, were placed alongside the casket while other wreaths were carried in an attached car (at right). This photo may have been taken when his body was being transported to Saint-Quentin.

(though admittedly, they are not a "pusher type" but are Caudrons). First, a Caudron GIV from *Esc.* C202, piloted by *MdL.* Louis Neel, returned to its base at Villers-Bretonneux that day with a mortally wounded observer, *Sous-Lt.* Jean Montpetit. It is possible that they had been attacked by Wintgens near Rancourt but had managed to escape. Another

Above & Below: Two scenes shortly before and during the funeral service.

This Page: The first photo shows Wintgens' undraped casket (white with a black cloth on top) being loaded onto a horse-drawn gun carriage outside the church. The next captures the procession, led by *Lt.* Walter Höhndorf carrying the dead man's *Ordenskissen*, as it wends its way through Saint-Quentin's streets to the cemetery. Behind Höhndorf are *Oblt.* Ernst von Althaus (left), *Oblt.* Hans-Joachim Buddecke (center) and *Lt.* Wilhelm Frankl (right) as well as NCOs from *FFA* 23 carrying the funeral wreaths. The third image has the chaplain saying a few words as the casket is lowered into its grave and the attendees salute. Althaus and Buddecke are the two men seen just to the left of the chaplain, and Höhndorf and Frankl are the two men just to the right of him. The final scene is of *Hptm.* Hermann Palmer, CO of *FFA* 23, doffing his service cap at the head of Wintgens' grave. Frankl and Höhndorf are at far left. The tall man in the background, sixth from the right, is *Vzfw.* Josef Veltjens, who would earn his *Pour le Mérite* on 16 August 1918.

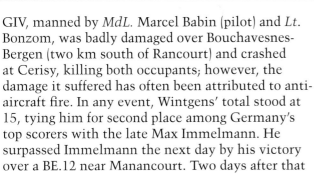

GIV, manned by *MdL.* Marcel Babin (pilot) and *Lt.* Bonzom, was badly damaged over Bouchavesnes-Bergen (two km south of Rancourt) and crashed at Cerisy, killing both occupants; however, the damage it suffered has often been attributed to anti-aircraft fire. In any event, Wintgens' total stood at 15, tying him for second place among Germany's top scorers with the late Max Immelmann. He surpassed Immelmann the next day by his victory over a BE.12 near Manancourt. Two days after that

he brought down a Nieuport Scout near Beaumetz. His final conquests, a "double" once again, were a BE.12 and Martinsyde G100 that he shot down on 24 September near Flesquières to bring his official total to 19. He was now Germany's second most successful ace, behind only the great Oswald Boelcke who had 28 victories.

Fate, in the highly capable form of French ace Alfred Heurtaux of Spa3, caught up to Wintgens on 25 September 1916 over Villers-Carbonnel.

Above: A closer view of Wintgens' grave at Saint-Quentin. This and other pictures of the *Pour le Mérite*-shaped wreath in the foreground tell us that it mimicked the real decoration's writing on its arms as well as the eagles between them.

Heurtaux, who was flying the new Spad VII fighter that day, reportedly recalled that he "dived single-handed to attack a flight of seven single-seaters flying in vee formation. Choosing the leader, reckoning that he would be safest in the middle of the enemy formation, he fired only five rounds before his opponent fell. Later it was discovered that his victim was the German ace Kurt Wintgens."[25] An official report from Supreme Headquarters stated: "On the morning of 25 September, *Lt.* Wintgens took off on an important mission in his airplane. The weather was clear, almost cloudless. Suddenly, enemy fliers appeared in superior strength behind

Above: Wintgen's coffin lies in state before the altar of St. Marien Church in Minden. Though his Ordenskissen (see closeup) is different than that used in St. Quentin, it displays the same decorations. (photo courtesy of Kommunalarchiv Minden, Bildsammlung D/Wintgens)

Facing Page Top & Bottom and Left: The funeral procession leaves St. Marien Church and marches along Marienstrasse toward the city's Nordfriedhof cemetery. *Lt.* Walter Höhndorf carried Wintgens' *Ordenskissen* and can be seen doing so at the head of the procession in the third photo (right). (photos courtesy of Kommunalarchiv Minden, Bildsammlung D/Wintgens)

Above & Below: *Lt*. Walter Höhndorf holds his friend's *Ordenskissen* at graveside during the ceremony at Nordfriedhof. (photos courtesy of Kommunalarchiv Minden, Bildsammlung D/Wintgens)

Above & Right: Wintgens' grave in Nordfriedhof. The closeup of his *Ordenskissen* shows the upward bow in the center of his *Pour le Mérite* (at the top of the pillow) that indicates that he had been wearing it when he crashed. (photos courtesy of Kommunalarchiv Minden, Bildsammlung D/Wintgens)

his machine from the direction of the sun where its bright light blinded him to their approach. Before *Lt.* Wintgens could make them out in the flood of light, he was caught in the combined fire of their machine guns. His motor and petrol tank were hit and his airplane fell uncontrolled from a height of 3900 meters into the depths below, just behind the German lines. The plane somersaulted upon impact with the earth. *Lt.* Wintgens, though practically unscathed, was dead."[26] Hans-Joachim Buddecke further elaborated in a letter dated 29 September: "One of the main elevator spars was shot through and broke like Höhndorf's and Berthold's, and he crashed. Wintgens himself did not show any gunshot wounds."[27]

Wintgens' remains were recovered and brought to Saint-Quentin for burial. On 27 September, services were held for him in one of the city's churches, after which his coffin was placed on a horse-drawn gun carriage for transport through the city's streets to one of its cemeteries. Behind the casket walked *Lt.*

Walter Höhndorf, carrying his friend's *Ordenskissen* (pillow displaying his decorations), accompanied by fellow *Pour le Mérite* holders *Oblt.* Ernst von Althaus, *Oblt.* Hans-Joachim Buddecke, *Lt.* Wilhelm Frankl, and a long procession of officers and soldiers. The ceremony attracted a great deal of attention, even as far away as the United States, where one newspaper there reported: "While fellow airmen wheeled their machines overhead and dropped wreaths of flowers upon his coffin, Lieut. Wintgens, next to Capt. Boelcke, the most successful German aviator flying in the west and chief competitor of the ill-fated Lieut. Immelmann, was borne to his last resting place. He had been killed in an air battle late in September. Lieut. Wintgens' burial was one of the most dramatic episodes in the history of the little French city, which has had its fill of the kind of drama that war brings. It was attended by almost every military person quartered in St. Quentin, and by a large number of civilians as well. The interment was in the local cemetery by special wish of the dead flier, who had asked that in case he fell he should be buried as near as possible to the scene of his death. After a heart-rending service in the little evangelical church here, Wintgens' body, in a black and white coffin smothered in floral offerings, was placed on a gun carriage and carried to the cemetery. Behind the coffin walked three fellow aviators, who with Wintgens have won the coveted order *Pour le Merite* – Baron Althaus, First Lieut. Buddecke, who has been flying for the Turkish army, and Lieut. Frankl. At the head of the funeral procession marched an honor company. Near the coffin was Wintgens' closest friend, the flier Lieut. Hoehndorf, who was the only witness to Wintgens' death, and who carried the many orders that had been conferred on the famous aviator since the beginning of the war. In the procession behind the gun carriage were representatives of the commanding general, and hundreds of representatives of the various flying corps of the many German armies, all of whom had known and appreciated Wintgens and his exceptional ability as an aviator. At the cemetery, while a comrade of the dead lieutenant spoke a few final words, two aviator friends of the deceased who had followed the funeral procession in their aeroplanes, let their machines volplane to within a short distance of the ground and let fall floral wreaths, and then opened up with their machine guns the crushing military salute of three volleys for the dead."[28]

Wintgens' body was exhumed and removed to Minden for reburial in the town's Nordfriedhof cemetery on 5 March 1917. The 1 April 1917 edition of *Die Luftflotte* (4, p.79) announced: "The interment of airman *Lt.* Wintgens (fallen on 25 September) recently took place in Minden following the transportation of the hero's corpse from France. Among the numerous mourners in attendance were the deceased's mother and sister, Hannover's officer corps, many flying officers and representatives of various authorities. Superintendent Graefe delivered the eulogy. Airman *Lt.* Höhndorf, who had fought alongside the fallen one during his last battle, carried the deceased's many medals on the way to the cemetery. Minden's citizenry lined the path to the cemetery. *Hptm.* Krüger, commander of an airship, spoke at the grave. A company of honor of Hannover's military airmen rendered the last honors to the dead hero."

Endnotes

[1] My thanks to air historian Manfred Thiemeyer for this information. Brother Max, who served with distinction in World War I as a *Hauptmann* in Africa, contracted typhus and allowed himself to be captured by Belgian forces on 23 May 1917 in order to find treatment. British newspapers reported that he was so respected by his opponents that he was allowed to retain his sword. He died as a retired *Major* in 1925.

[2] See Zuerl, *Pour-le-mérite Flieger*, p.478. For the English translations of Wintgens' letters used herein, see Jeffrey Sands, "The Forgotten Ace" in *Cross & Cockade* 26:2, pp.83–104.

[3] Wintgens was referring to Mario (Mauricio) Scherff and Richard Schmidt. His use of "*Kanonen*" (literally "cannons") at this stage of the war, when there were neither German "aces" (as the term is often translated) nor machine guns mounted on German fighter planes, gives us insight into the term's original meaning: "big guns" or "big shots" as in famous persons.

[4] Grosz, *Fokker E.I/II*, p.9.

[5] Fokker demonstrated his first E.II (M14, *Werknummer* 257) to Crown Prince Wilhelm and other military officials at Stenay on 13 June.

[6] The report also said Boutiny was armed only with a carbine and not a machine gun.

[7] The report dates the action to 9 July, not 10 July as indicated by Wintgens.

[8] *Hptm.* Friedrich Jägerhuber, CO of *FFA* 6b, flew in the battle with an *Oblt.* Häfner as his observer. Jägerhuber and *Lt.* Oskar Schinnerer (Wintgens' erstwhile pilot) died together in a car crash at Réding (near Sarrebourg) a little over a week later on 17 July 1915.

[9] This probably was a reference to Eugene Gilbert or Adolphe Pégoud (or both), who belonged to *Esc.* MS49, based at Fontaine. By the time of Wintgens' letter, Gilbert and Pégoud had combined for three confirmed MS49 victories – two of which were *FFA* 48 aircraft (on 17 June and 9 July).

[10] Previously, the honor had been afforded to Max Immelmann's victory of 1 August 1915.

[11] My thanks to aero historian Reinhard Kastner, who supplied this information.

[12] Franks, Bailey & Duiven, *Casualties of the German Air Service*, p.182.

[13] Grosz, *Fokker E.IV*, p.1.

[14] Oswald Boelcke and Max Immelmann, with respective scores of six and seven, were given their *Ehrenbechers* on Christmas Day 1915.

[15] The address was incorrectly spelled as "Burdingshofen" in *Cross & Cockade* 26:2, p.100.

[16] Other photos attest to the fact that sometime after this, "*durch Ltn. Höhndorf am 17.1.16*" ("by Lt. Höhndorf on 17 January 1916") was added to the painted phrase.

[17] Walter Höhndorf's June 1916 victories also fell well south and east of Haumont-prés-Samogneux: 2 June – west of Morhange, 17 June – south of Château-Salins, 22 June – Lembach, 25 June – Raucourt.

[18] *Sharks Among Minnows*, pp.104-05.

[19] The Farman may have been crewed by *Sergeant* Pierre Lamielle and *Lieutenant* Amédée Pluven of MF7, though French records indicate that they were brought down by antiaircraft fire.

[20] His comrade, *Lt*. Walter Höhndorf, was sent to *KEK* Vaux.

[21] See Bronnenkant, *Imperial German Eagles 1*, pp.146–47.

[22] See O'Connor, *Aviation Awards of Imperial Germany 6*, p.313.

[23] *El Schahin*, pp.92–93.

[24] *Fw*. Leopold Rudolf Reimann was sent to *Jasta* 2 (Boelcke) on 1 September 1916.

[25] Robertson, *Air Aces of the 1914–1918 War*, p.70.

[26] For the original German text, see *Flugsport* 21, p.563 or Bronnenkant, *Imperial German Eagles 3*, p.48.

[27] O'Connor, *Aviation Awards of Imperial Germany 4*, p.232. Neither Buddecke's letter nor the Supreme Headquarters report (when read carefully) supports later accounts like the one presented in *Die Luftflotte's* 1 November edition (11, p.151) that added: "his petrol tank was hit by an explosive bullet, blew up and started to burn." The use of explosive bullets during the early years of the war was an extremely controversial topic that was covered extensively in newspapers and led to heated recriminations from both sides. Thus this addition may have been an embellishment designed to further incite the public over their hero's loss.

[28] *The Lowell Sun*, 17 Nov 1916.

Above: A picture of Kurt Wintgens when he was a boy in Minden. (photo courtesy of Kommunalarchiv Minden, Bildsammlung D/Wintgens)

Right: A grainy photograph of the wreckage of MF58's Farman 3009, manned by *Adj.* Semelin and *Sous-Lt.* Gallon, brought down near Blâmont on 23 June 1916. Evidently, they were Wintgens' seventh victory.

Wintgens – The Aircraft

Fokker M.5L monoplane, M.7 biplane, M.8 monoplane, M.10 biplane
(March–mid-June 1915)

Writing from Fokker's factory and school at Schwerin-Görries on 25 March 1915, Kurt Wintgens exclaimed: "And now, first of all, the new Fokker monoplanes, in one word 'the machine.' Maybe you have already seen a picture of them, monoplanes and biplanes. I am being trained on both. The monoplane is like the Morane type 14 resp. 18 m² qua wing with 80 hp Gnôme (Gnom – that means *'geht nie ohne Monteur,'* or 'never goes without a mechanic'). Speed about 140 km/hr, climb 1000m in three minutes,

and so lightly-built that in every position, even close down to earth, the machine can be flattened out. Fokker himself performs the most dangerous stunts. A looping impresses no one anymore. Just that enormous lightness (yet 6–7x safety) makes flying in it so nice. And, of course, crashes mostly are less dangerous than in heavier machines. When, for instance, in a heavy LVG or AEG biplane a certain glide angle is passed, the central point of pressure goes to the last third part of the wings and the machine is no longer obedient to the elevator, while with the Fokker mono- and biplanes, the machine can be rightened from every, even vertical, position. Most of the biplanes are being built now with the Mercedes engine so that one can make long country

W1

W2

W1: *Lt.* Kurt Wintgens in his "looping-machine" – a Fokker M.5L monoplane. Note the cutouts at the wing roots and accomodation behind Wintgens for a passenger.

W2: Kurt Wintgens, sitting in the cockpit of a Fokker M.8/A.I monoplane, is congratulated by men on the ground.

flights that are not so advisable with the Gnôme. All machines, by the way, have a stick for steering." At this time, Fokker's stable of 80 hp aircraft was comprised of the M.5 and M.8 monoplanes and M.7 biplane. The M.5L had a wing surface area of 18 m² as noted above, and we have a snapshot of Wintgens in one that was almost certainly taken at Döberitz where he wrote on 27 May 1915: "Enclosed are two photographs showing me in my looping-machine. It is the first time I had myself photographed in an aeroplane." W2 is a snapshot of Wintgens in an M.8, so we know he flew this type as well. On 16 April 1915, Wintgens referred again to Fokker's "biplane": "Yesterday afternoon something very tragic happened here. Our great 'Kanone' Scherff crashed with his mechanic from 1200m in a biplane. Apparently the wings broke off. I witnessed the fall from start to finish. It was lucky in that they fell into the water some 20m from the coast, which lessened the impact much... As a consequence of this crash, which followed another of the same type some days earlier, the Fokker biplane will probably leave the scene." Here Wintgens was talking about M.7 wing failures during test flights by Alexander von Bismarck and Mario Scherff, so it must have been one of the biplanes mentioned in his letters.[1] But

he also wrote on 16 April: "The first solo flight is a very strange experience when those 100 hp fly away with you, especially with our unbelievably sensitive crates." This and his earlier reference to most of the biplanes being built with Mercedes engines points to the M.10 biplane which indeed used a 100 hp rotary engine and was also modified to employ a 100 hp Mercedes.

Fokker E.I 5/15
(Late June–? 1915)

Owing to his strong relationship with Anthony Fokker, Kurt Wintgens was the third airman after Otto Parschau (1/15) and Oswald Boelcke (3/15) to receive one of Fokker's new E.I fighting machines. His bore the serial number E.I 5/15 and we have several photos of it – both before and after its delivery to Wintgens. E.I 5/15 began its life as a Fokker A.III (*Werknummer* 198). It originally sported wings mounted high on the fuselage with openings at their roots to provide downward viewing[2]. After being fitted with a Parabellum LMG 14 machine gun, the starboard cowling was modified to accomodate onboard ammunition, the wing was lowered, and its root openings were filled in. It retained its *Werknummer* but was redesignated E.I

W3: A close-up view of Fokker E.I 5/15's cockpit while the plane was still at the factory at Schwerin-Görries. Note the headrest used to align the pilot with the Parabellum machine gun's correct line of fire. The somewhat elaborate means by which the machine gun's ammunition belt was enclosed and guided is also quite visible. (photo courtesy of Greg VanWyngarden)

W4–7: Multiple views of Fokker E.I 5/15 when its fuselage and underbelly did not yet display the stains and discoloration of repeated use. Wintgens is seated in its cockpit in the second and third pictures. (photos courtesy of Greg VanWyngarden)

5/15 and shipped from the Fokker factory on 24 June 1915.[3] It made its way south to Mannheim where Wintgens tested it and then flew it via Strasbourg to *FFA* 6b's base at Sarrebourg-Bühl. He wasted little time in using it and on 1 July 1915 became the first Fokker *Eindecker* pilot to shoot up and force down an enemy plane. He forced another to land on 4 July but it was not until 15 July, after he had moved to *FFA* 48 near Mühlhausen, that he was finally granted

an official victory – again the first of its kind for an *Eindecker* pilot. W3 is a closeup of E.I 5/15's cockpit shortly before it was shipped to Wintgens. W4–7 are pictures of E.I 5/15 – some with Wintgens in the cockpit – when it was still relatively new (i.e., the plane exhibits few signs of staining, particularly along the bottom edge of the fuselage). W8 displays an older 5/15 with different markings sometime after Wintgens' departure from *FFA* 48 and return to *FFA*

6b in the summer of 1915. We do not know how long Wintgens continued to use 5/15. It is reasonable to assume that he would have upgraded to one or more of the more powerful E.II and E.III (100 hp) models before his acceptance of E.IV 124/15 in January 1916; however, we have no photos or other records to confirm this.

Fokker E.IV 124/15
(January–September 1916)
Like the earlier E.I, Wintgens was the third airman after Otto Parschau (122/15) and Oswald Boelcke

(123/15) to be given a 160 hp Fokker E.IV. His E.IV 124/15 was shipped and delivered to him in January 1916 and W9–10 capture it and its proud owner on a snow-covered field when it was still relatively new. We can see that though it shared the same early machine gun arrangement (offset to starboard as opposed to centered) as its two predecessors, it was unlike them in that its cowling and metal paneling aft of the engine had been reduced in size. The caption on the reverse of W11 identifies it as Wintgens' E.IV after an emergency landing. The attributes cited above confirm this identification;

W8: Wintgens sits in E.I 5/15 after his return to *FFA* 6b from *FFA* 48. Reinhard Kastner (*Das Propellerblatt 2*, pp.83–96) tells us that the markings seen here were typical of *FFA* 48's army group aircraft: black and white fuselage bands and a black rudder. *FFA* 6b's *Lt.* Theodor Triendl is second from the left.

and since what can be seen of the serial number is still reasonably legible, the photo may have originated in the late winter or early spring of 1916. W13–16 is a sequence of action photos showing Wintgens preparing to fly 124/15. The fact that Wintgens is wearing the *Pour le Mérite* he had been awarded on 1 July dates the sequence to sometime after that. On 22 June 1916, Wintgens wrote that his E.IV's damaged engine, which was being sent back to Oberursel for repair, "has reasonably earned its cooper up in the factory, for now it has downed one Clerget, two Le Rhône and lastly a 16-valve Renault... which was my sixth." This confirms that he achieved his fourth (Nieuport XII with a 110 hp Clerget), fifth (Caudron GIV with two 80 hp Le Rhône rotaries), and sixth (a Renault-powered Farman) victories in 124/15.[5] He apparently used another E-type for his seventh on 23 June because his E.IV's engine had just been returned to Oberursel for repair and eyewitnesses to the two actions that are candidates for this victory (Victor Chapman's Nieuport and an MF58 Farman) both still mentioned Fokker aircraft. We cannot be sure what plane he was in for his eighth on 30 June but circumstantial evidence points to the Halberstadt D.II fighter he was photographed with below. His mount when he shot down his ninth on 19 July could have been either the same Halberstadt D.II or E.IV

W9–10: *Lt.* Kurt Wintgens, clad in his winter flight gear, poses alongside his new Fokker E.IV 124/15. Like the photos of his E.I 5/15, E.IV 124/15 shows few signs of wear in these images.

W10

W11

W11: The back of this snapshot defines its subject as *"Notlandung von Lt. Wintgens"* ("Emergency landing by *Lt.* Wintgens"). Upon close examination, several attributes including the offset machine guns and identification plate confirm the identification.

W12

W12: Fokker E.IV 124/15 is decorated with a wreath bearing the number "12" at its center in celebration of Wintgen's victory of 30 July 1916. We know it was 124/15 because of the offest machine guns (see blowup).

W13–15: A series of pictures taken at the same time of Kurt Wintgens preparing to fly his Fokker E.IV 124/15. We know it was this airplane because of two unique features: the curved metal panels where the forward landing gear struts attached to the fuselage and the slightly curved (as opposed to straight) panel just below the cockpit. The first shot shows him inspecting the nose, perhaps contemplating why a censor had brushed out a machine gun (its ghostly white imprint is nevertheless visible). The final two have him standing alongside the machine and clamboring into the cockpit (with a Halberstadt fighter in the background). At this point, some different features appear on the aircraft. First, the fuselage insignia had been repainted using a newer style cross patee (note too how unblemished the insignia appears compared to the heavily stained fuselage). Second, the starboard wing insignia's cross patee (see W15) is no longer set against a solid white background but is only thinly outlined in white. This may have been due to either a complete overpainting of the wing or the substitution of a new one. Note too what appears to have been a bullet hole patch at the bottom of the wing insignia.

W16: Another snapshot of Wintgens with E.IV 124/15. It was taken sometime between W9–11 and W13–15 because the plane's fuselage still bears the older style – though now quite worn – national insignia. The fuselage stain pattern is also identical to, though less heavy than, that displayed in W14. Note the two bullet hole patches that are visible on the fuselage side just aft of the cockpit (under the mechanic's knee). Wintgens is wearing his *Pour le Mérite* in this and the prior three photos, which tells us that (i) they occurred after his receipt of the award on 1 July 1916 and (ii) he was not averse to wearing the decoration in combat.

W17–18: In the first picture, *Lt.* Kurt Wintgens poses in front of his Halberstadt D.II that had been adorned by garlands and a wreath in celebration of a special event that most likely was his *Pour le Mérite*-qualifying eighth victory on 30 June 1916. The second (following page) captures him (second from left), *Generaloberst* Ludwig von Falkenhausen (third from left), *Lt.* Walter Höhndorf (second from right), and two other men who all appeared in another group portrait taken shortly after Falkenhausen had bestowed the *Pour le Mérite* upon Wintgens.

124/15, because eyewitnesses to his tenth success just two days later reported that plane as having been attacked by two Fokkers (flown by Wintgens and *Vzfw.* Wolfgang Heinemann).[6] We have no information on the aircraft he used for victories 11 and 13-15, but we have W12's testimony that he used E.IV 124/15 for his 12th victory. His 16th victim, 2Lt. Colin Elphinston, also reported that a Fokker brought him down on 15 September[7]. The jury is out when it comes to his 17th and 18th successes, but the survivor of his 19th on 24 September – 2Lt. Ernest Wingfield – stated upon his repatriation in 1918 that a Leutnant Wintgens had shot him down in a Fokker.[8] Finally, we have *Oblt.* Hans-Joachim Buddecke's letter of 29 September 1916 that specified: "Today we must bury our good man, Wintgens. He was surprised while flying a Fokker Eindecker E.IV (160 hp, No.1)."[9] We have no indication that it was anything other than 124/15.

Halberstadt D.II
(June–? 1916)
The first Halberstadt D.II (120 hp Mercedes D.II engine) and D.III (120 hp Argus As.II engine) fighters began arriving at the Front in June 1916. One D.II

intended for *Oblt.* Max Immelmann arrived at his Douai airbase on 22 June just four days after his death and was test flown by *Hptm.* Oswald Boelcke (who was there for Immelmann's funeral) instead. Another went to Kurt Wintgens, as seen in W17–18. W17 captures Wintgens' Mercedes-powered D.II after it had been decorated in a manner that usually signified a special victory. We know that Wintgens used Fokker aircraft for his first seven victories. He was awarded the *Pour le Mérite* the day after his eighth, but there is no sign of the decoration that was "to be worn at all times" in W17.[10] Therefore, it almost certainly is a picture of Wintgens and the Halberstadt D.II he must have used to bring down his eighth opponent on 30 June. Wintgens is again without his *Pour le Mérite* in W18, where he is standing with many of the same men posed in what is believed to have been that decoration's investiture picture (see p.46). W19–20 are two more portraits of Wintgens with the same plane, again without his *Pour le Mérite*. Whether he ever flew it or any other Halberstadt fighter after the summer of 1916 is currently unknown. He seemed to have preferred his Fokker E.IV despite its inferior flight capabilities when compared to the Halberstadt D.II. A D.II

W19–20: Two more familiar images of Wintgens (sans *Pour le Mérite*) with his Halberstadt D.II.

weakness that was often cited by German pilots was that it carried only one machine gun, so we might speculate that Wintgens favored the extra firepower and backup provided by the E.IV's second gun.

Endnotes

[1] Bismarck, though seriously injured, survived. Scherff recovered after a few weeks but his mechanic, Hoengen, reportedly died a year later.

[2] For a photograph of it, see Grosz, *Fokker E.I/II*, p.8.

[3] Grosz, *Fokker E.I/II*, p.9.

[4] See Grosz, *Fokker E.IV*, pp.9 and 13.

[5] The translation in *Cross & Cockade* 26:2, p.103 has "16-cylinder" instead of 16-valve. A 16-cylinder engine was virtually unheard of at the time (Bugatti developed a U-16 engine in 1915/1916 that apparently was not used on an airplane until 1917) and there is no record of Renault ever having produced one during World War I. Non-rotary powered Farmans normally used an 8-cylinder or 12-cylinder Renault engine. Wintgens was pretty techno-savvy, so it would have been strange for him to have mistaken an 8- or 12-cylinder engine for one with 16. Therefore, it has been assumed that the translation was incorrect and "16-valve" was chosen as the most reasonable substitute.

[6] Admittedly, it is also possible that he was flying another E-type; but since there are photos of him using E.IV 124/15 after 1 July (W11–15), it seems to be a more likely candidate.

[7] Franks, *Sharks Among Minnows*, p.139.

[8] Ibid., p.141.

[9] O'Connor, *Aviation Awards of Imperial Germany 4*, p.232. Exactly what Buddecke meant by "No.1" is a mystery. No E.IV was assigned such a serial or works number. Did Buddecke mistakenly believe that 124/15, one of the earliest E.IVs produced, was the first of its kind?

[10] Wintgens, like several other pilots, appears to have followed those instructions even when up in the air. The W13–16 photo series demonstrates that he wore it under his flight gear; and the *Pour le Mérite* displayed on his *Ordenskissen* at his funeral service (see p.51) shows signs of damage that probably occurred when he crashed to earth.

Above: A pleasing portrait of Wintgens that was signed by him on the back and dated 14 September 1916 – less than two weeks before he was killed.

Right: Candid snapshot of Wintgens that was taken when he visited the crash site of his 13th victim.

Above: Wintgens (center of car, facing camera) and *Oblt.* Hans-Joachim Buddecke (back seat of car, closest to camera) at an airfield together in the late summer of 1916.

Right: Wintgens and the same pilot officer seen in the front seat of the car in the picture above. (photo courtesy of Kommunalarchiv Minden, Bildsammlung D/Wintgens)

Below: Kurt Wintgens poses with several friends or associates.

Wintgens – Military Service

Significant Dates

1 Aug 1894	born in Bad Neustadt an der Saale
early 1913	entered *Telegraphen-Bataillon* Nr.2
Aug 1914	observer with air service
Oct 1914	back with *Telegraphen-Bataillon* Nr.2
Feb 1915	pilot's training began at *Flieger-Bataillon* 1
Mar 1915	assigned to Fokker school at Schwerin-Görries
May/Jun 1915	earned Pilot's Badge
late Jun 1915	assigned to *Feldflieger-Abteilung* 6b
mid-Jul 1915	assigned to *Feldflieger-Abteilung* 48
1 Jul 1915	first claimed victory for himself and any Fokker *Eindecker* pilot
15 Jul 1915	first official victory for himself and any Fokker *Eindecker* pilot
early Aug 1915	assigned to *Feldflieger-Abteilung* 67*
Sep 1915	assigned to *Feldflieger-Abteilung* 6b
Oct 1915	assigned to *Feldflieger-Abteilung* 67*
early 1916	assigned to *Feldflieger-Abteilung* 12, then possibly *Feldflieger-Abteilung* 67 and/or *Fokkerstaffel* Falkenhausen*
1 Jul 1916	awarded *Pour le Mérite*
mid-Jul 1916	assigned to *KEK* Bertincourt or *KEK* Vaux
22 Aug 1916	assigned to *Jasta* 1
late Aug 1916?	assigned to *Jasta* 4**
mid-Sep 1916	assigned to *Jasta* 1
24 Sep 1916	final victory (#19)
25 Sep 1916	killed in action
29 Sep 1916	buried in Saint-Quentin
Mar 1917	reburied in Minden

*based on evidence presented on pages 42-46
**based on evidence presented on page 49

Service Units

1913–Jul 1914	*Telegraphen-Bataillon* Nr.2
Aug–Sep 1914	unknown air unit
Oct 1914–Jan 1915	*Telegraphen-Bataillon* Nr.2
Feb 1915	*Flieger-Bataillon* 1
Mar–early May 1915	Fokker School
mid-May–mid-Jun 1915	*Flieger-Bataillon* 1
late Jun–early Jul 1915	*Feldflieger-Abteilung* 6b
mid-Jul–early Aug 1915	*Feldflieger-Abteilung* 48
early Aug 1915–Sep 1915	*Feldflieger-Abteilung* 67*
Sep 1915	*Feldflieger-Abteilung* 6b
Oct 1915	*Feldflieger-Abteilung* 67*
Nov 1915–early Jan 1916	?
mid-Jan–? 1916	*Feldflieger-Abteilung* 12
?–mid-Jul 1916	*Feldflieger-Abteilung* 67 (and/or *Fokkerstaffel* Falkenhausen)
late Jul–late Aug 1916	*KEK* Bertincourt or *KEK* Vaux
23 Aug– ?	*Jasta* 1
?–mid-Sep 1916	*Jasta* 4
mid-Sep–25 Sep 1916	*Jasta* 1

Awards

early 1915	Iron Cross, 2nd Class – Prussia
May/Jun 1915	Pilot's Badge – Germany
early Jan 1916	*Ehrenbecher* – Germany
18–30 Jun 1916	Royal Hohenzollern House Order, Knight's Cross with Swords – Prussia
1 Jul 1916	*Pour le Mérite* – Prussia
19 Jul 1916	Albert Order, Knight 2nd Class with Swords – Saxony
unknown	Iron Cross, 1st Class – Prussia (possibly after 1st victory, 15 Jul1915)
unknown	Military Merit Order, 4th Class with Swords – Bavaria (prior to PLM)

Below: Another view of Wintgens' 10th victim, brought down on 21 July 1916 (see page 48).

Left: Wintgens inspects the crash site of his 16th victim, BE.12 6583, flown by Lt. C. Elphinston of RFC No.21 Squadron (wounded and taken prisoner).

Wintgens – Victory List

No.	Date	Aircraft	Location, Unit & Crew *
1	15 Jul 1915	Morane Parasol	near Col de la Schlucht – ?
2	?	?	?
3	9 Aug	Voisin	near Gondrexange – Esc VB112: *MdL.* Louis Pasco, *Sgt.* Phillipe Toureille (b-KIA)
4	20 May 1916	Nieuport XII	near Château-Salins – Esc N68: *MdL.* Leon Cesar Léon Beauchamps (WIA/POW), *Sous-Lt.* Debacker (KIA)
5	21 May	Caudron GIV	near Château-Salins – Esc C43: *Brig.* Vincent, *Sous-Lt.* René Gauthier (b-KIA)
6	17 Jun	Farman	near Bezange-la-Grande – MF70: *Lt.* Brunel and *Sous-Lt.* Pierre Hemand (b-KIA)
7	23 Jun	Farman 3009	near Blâmont – MF58: Adj. Jacques Semelin, *Sous-Lt.* Gallon (b-KIA)
8	30 Jun	Farman	southwest of Château-Salins – MF7: *Sgt.* Pierre Lamielle, *Lt.* Amedée Pluven? (b-KIA)
9	19 Jul	Sopwith Strutter A386	near Arras – RFC 70: Lt. HR Hele-Shaw, 2Lt. RC Oakes (b-KIA)
10	21 Jul	BE.2c 2100	near Aubigny-au-Bac – RFC 12: 2Lt. RM Wilson-Browne (POW/DOW)
11	21 Jul	Morane N A128	near Achiet-le-Petit – RFC 60: Cpt. NA Browning-Patersen (KIA)
12	30 Jul	Martinsyde G100 7471	east of Péronne – RFC 27: 2Lt. LN Graham (WIA/POW)
13	2 Aug	Morane BB 5177	near Poeuilly – RFC 60: Lt. JAN Ormsby (POW/DOW), 2Lt. HJ Newton (KIA)
14	14 Sep	Nieuport	near Bussu – ?
15	14 Sep	"pusher type" Caudron GIV?	north of Rancourt –Esc C202, *MdL.* Neel (OK), *Sous-Lt.* J. Monpetit (KIA)? OR Esc.?, *MdL.* Marcel Babin, *Lt.* Bonzom (b-KIA)
16	15 Sep	BE.12 6583	near Manancourt – RFC 21: Lt. C Elphinston (WIA/POW)
17	17 Sep	Nieuport scout	near Beaumetz – Esc N37: *Cpl.* Georges Marcowitz (KIA) OR *Sgt.* George de Geuser (KIA)
18	24 Sep	BE.12 6579	near Flesquières – RFC 19: 2Lt. G Edwards (KIA)
19	24 Sep	Martinsyde G100 7498	near Ribécourt-la-Tour – RFC 27: 2Lt. EN Wingfield (POW)

*pilot listed first
b-   both occupants
DOW   died of wounds

KIA   killed in action
POW   prisoner of war
WIA   wounded in action

Above & Right: Wintgens poses alongside the remains of his 18th victory, BE.12 6579. The corpse of its occupant, the unfortunate 2Lt. E.N. Wingfield of RFC No.19 Squadron, is being extricated from the wreck in the second image.

Max *Ritter* von Mulzer

Above: Max *Ritter* von Mulzer sat for this formal portrait (and several others) at Karl Müller's studio in Memmingen during his only home leave following his award of the *Pour le Mérite* on 8 July 1916. Here we see all the decorations he earned save one – the Military Max-Joseph Order, Knight's Cross – that was bestowed upon him in the field after his return to the Front. They are: *Pour le Mérite* (at his neck); Military Merit Order, 4th Class with Swords; Iron Cross 2nd Class; Royal Hohenzollern House Order, Knight's Cross with Swords, Hamburg Hanseatic Cross; Friedrich Cross, 2nd Class (medals bar, left to right); Iron Cross, 1st Class, Bavarian Pilot's Badge (pinned underneath).

Mulzer – The Man

Youth and Early Career

Hospital physician Dr. Max Mulzer and his wife Katharina Maria (née Zillibiller) welcomed their first child, Max Georg, on 9 July 1893 when the couple lived in the Bavarian town of Kimratshofen (north of Kempten). The Mulzers moved farther east to Dietmannsried where Max was joined by a little sister. Described by a local publication as "a small beauty with large dark eyes and a lively manner," she died in a tragic accident at an early age; and it was said that up until his own death, Max "often spoke of his dead little sister with great longing."[1] Brothers Albert and Josef arrived next, and in February 1906 the family relocated north to Memmingen, where Max had been attending secondary school since 1903. Max loved animals and horses in particular, which led to his decision in 1908 to enter the Cadet Corps – an organization that offered a high school education in a military environment – with the goal of becoming a cavalry officer. He graduated with average grades and was sent as a *Fähnrich* (officer candidate) to Bavaria's 8th *Chevaulegers-Regiment* (Light Horse Cavalry Regiment) at Dillingen an der Donau on 10 July 1914. After the war broke out, he traveled to the Front with the regiment and performed several long-range reconnaissance patrols (during one of which

Right: A childhood portrait of Max Mulzer and his little sister.

Below: Mulzer shows his early penchant for riding as he sits astride a horse in the garden of his family's home in Dietmannsried.

his horse was reportedly shot out from under him) that led to his being awarded the Iron Cross 2nd Class on 10 October.[2] He participated in the fighting around Badonviller, Sarrebourg and Nancy and was promoted to *Leutnant* on 13 December 1914.

Airman

Mulzer applied for entry into the *Fliegertruppe* (Army Air Service) and was sent on 20 August 1915 to Bavarian *Flieger-Ersatz-Abteilung* 1b at Schleissheim for pilot training. After completing his course in November, he was ordered to *Armee-Flug-Park* 6 at Valenciennes to await further disposition to the Front. On 13 December 1915, he was assigned to *Feldflieger-Abteilung* 4b but was then shifted in January 1916 to *Abwehrkommando* II, attached to *Feldflieger-Abteilung* 62 at La Brayelle airfield outside of Douai.[3] There he joined a unit that included Oswald Boelcke and Max Immelmann – the first German airmen to be awarded the *Pour le Mérite* that same month – and future stars Ernst Hess and Maximilian von Cossel.

Fighter Pilot

Oswald Boelcke was transferred out of *FFA* 62 on 21 January, but it appears that Immelmann took Mulzer under his wing and became both a mentor and friend to the young Bavarian. Immelmann had plenty of time to tutor Mulzer because he wrote that before 2 March: "No Englishman had been seen over Douai since February 5th."[4] On 13 March, Mulzer got in the thick of it: "I took off at 12 (noon) in company with another Fokker pilot, Lieutenant Mulzer, to keep order in the air further south... When I arrived, I saw a German biplane and another one about 100 metres above it... I flew up and finally spotted the cockades. Now for it, I thought, and fired... peng... peng... peng... and then, after a few shots, my gun jammed. I turned away from him, cleared the gun and made another attack. Mulzer had arrived by then, and he joined in. So now we concentrated our fire on him. I sent out 700 rounds of continuous fire, while Mulzer let off 100. Bump! Down he went like a stone into the depths and came to earth near Serre village."[5] *FFA* 62's commanding officer, *Hptm.* Hermann Kastner, reported: "*Lt.* Immelmann and *Lt.* Mulzer, who had started a patrol flight at 12:50, saw an enemy English biplane to the west of Bapaume at about 3000 meters altitude and attacked it. After a few turns their height amounted to only 2700 meters when Immelmann had to break off from the fight because of a gun jam. After it was eliminated, the two officers renewed their attack, climbed up to about 2200 meters afterwards and saw the hostile flier falling to earth. The enemy appeared to have

Above: Max Mulzer and comrades at Schleissheim in August/September 1915. Front row (left to right): *Lt.* Hans Friedlaender, *Lt.* Walter Killiani, *Lt.* Karl Wölfel, *Lt.* Maximilian Veith. Back row (left to right): unknown, *Lt.* Kurt Lämmle, *Lt.* Robert Moser, *Lt.* Karl Heussenstamm, Keilmeier, *Lt.* Friedrich Walther, Mulzer, *Lt.* Adolf Kuen. (photo courtesy of Tobias Weber)

had a machine gun on its wing since it occasionally tried to get behind the Fokker. The machine lies destroyed in Infantry Regiment 180's (2nd Army) section. More detailed information cannot be given yet, since strong enemy artillery fire is preventing any approach to the destroyed apparatus."[6] The next day, Supreme Headquarters announced: "An enemy airplane was finished off by *Lt.* Mulzer and *Lt.* Immelmann on 13 March 1916. The airplane was awarded to *Lt.* Immelmann. Because of his outstanding participation, *Lt.* Mulzer received the *Ehrenbecher* for the 'Victor in Air Combat' in accordance with the Chief of Field Aviation's decree no.14767."[7] Normally, the *Ehrenbecher* (a silver goblet engraved with the words "*Dem Sieger im Luftkampf*") was awarded to a pilot upon the occasion of his first victory, but this report indicates it could be given out under slightly different circumstances as well.

Mulzer's first official victory came on 30 March 1916, but not without considerable controversy. Two Fokker fighters piloted by *Lt.* Burkhard Lehmann and *Lt.* Otto Schmedes of *FFA* 32 attacked a group of RFC No.8 Squadron BE.2s near Bapaume. Their machine gun fire evidently killed the observer of BE.2c 2605, Airman 1st Class Arnold Walker, before Mulzer swooped in. The BE.2c eventually set down within German lines near Monchy-au-Bois where its wounded pilot, Lt. T.C. Wilson, was taken prisoner. All three Fokker pilots claimed the success. But Mulzer wrote a letter to *Maj.* Friedrich Stempel, *Stofl.* 6 (Aviation Staff Officer for the 6th Army),

Above: Mulzer finds himself in august company shortly after his arrival at *FFA* 62. This well-known photo was taken on 20 January 1916 as a farewell group shot for Boelcke, who left *FFA* 62 the next day. Front row (right to left): Salffner, Meding, *Lt.* Albert Oesterreicher, *Lt.* Oswald Boelcke, *Hptm.* Hermann Kastner (CO), *Lt.* Max Immelmann, von Krause, *Lt.* Ernst Hess. Back row (left to right): Mulzer, von Schilling, *Oblt.* Maximilian von Cossel, Fromme, *Oblt.* von Gusnar.

arguing that after the other two Fokkers' initial attack, the BE.2c with its lifeless observer had still turned under control toward its own lines – a sign that it was not yet finished – and that it was he who had administered the *coup de grâce*. Moreover, he had witnesses to this effect. On 27 April, almost one month after the event, Stempel's commission ruled that though Lehmann and Schmedes had played a significant part in bringing down the enemy plane, the final credit would go to Mulzer who had ensured its landing and capture. As consolation, however, *das Beutegeld* (the reward paid for captured aircraft) went to *FFA* 32.

Mulzer's native Bavaria did not wait for the commission's ruling and presented him with its Military Merit Order, 4th Class with Swords on 17 April. It evidently believed he had achieved at least one victory by this date.

Mulzer's next claim has often been listed as FE.2b 5210 of RFC No.25 Squadron, brought down about 25 miles northwest of Arras near Estaires on 23 April. Yet accounts by Dr. Ernst Sieverts and Max Immelmann confirm a different identification. Sieverts wrote: "A telephone orderly clicks his heels in front of our section leader [*Hptm.* Hermann Kastner] and announces: 'An enemy plane was shot down by a Fokker south of the Arras-to-Cambrai

road, near F[euchy].' Splendid! Who was the likely lucky one? Three are away, Immelmann, Mulzer and W[eber]. We guess. Most hold to Immelmann; secretly we hope that 'Maxl' Mulzer finally has an indisputable success this time. Up to now he has had swinish bad luck. Then a telephone orderly rushes up again: ` *Herr Hauptmann* is requested by *Lt.* Mulzer to come to the phone.' Hello! Does that confirm the message? The captain hurries to the telephone; we wait impatiently. The chief appears again, smiling: `Mulzer has just announced to me the shooting down of an enemy flier at the Front, south of Arras. He has landed but will take off again right away, because the hostile airplane is lying between the lines...' The telephone quickly rings again and Infantry Regiment No. __ confirms Mulzer's message. The airplane is completely smashed and lies right in front of the German trenches. Hurrah! It's a lucky day once again... Then one hears a subtle engine noise. We cock our heads. Is it a Fokker? There it is. Binoculars search the sky... There it is. It comes toward us in a steep gliding flight over the city. And then another one, quite nearby, coming from the Front. Both land nearly at the same time, roll on to their sheds. Mechanics run toward them, gather around to carefully escort the large birds. We go to the sheds to greet them. Mulzer speaks with his mechanic before he climbs from the seat in order to report his return to the section leader. I observe him and see that he is plainly embarrassed while reporting his success. Our 'Maxl' is over-modest. Calmly and objectively, as if describing something he had merely observed as a spectator, he provides information about the air combat... After his description one would think he had just been lucky. He fends off our congratulations, moves away and disappears as soon as the opportunity presents itself."[8] Immelmann, flying the second Fokker, believed it was his victory, however. He wrote: "On April 23rd I took off to fly a barrage with Lieutenant Mulzer, who is also a Fokker pilot of our section. After flying for an hour, we sighted an English biplane, which we attacked. Lieutenant Mulzer arrived a bit sooner and attacked him first. Then I came along too and fired about 120 rounds. We went on pursuing him until at last he landed at Monchy, near Arras. I was delighted at getting No.14."[9] Immelmann's biographer, brother Franz, omitted the next portion of Max's letter, which read: "But the Englishmen testified that the shot they got in their [petrol] tank came only during the first attack. So it therefore was Mulzer. Well, it doesn't matter."[10] But it did matter to someone in authority because, as we shall soon see, the victory that was awarded to Immelmann as his fourteenth seems to have somehow figured into Mulzer's official tally too.

Mulzer's next claim followed just three days later on 26 April. He and *Lt.* Albert Oesterreicher attacked RFC No.18 Squadron's FE.2b 5232 near Souchez.[11] Their fire wounded its observer, 2Lt. James Mitchell, and damaged the plane's controls, yet pilot 2nd Lt. Joseph C. Callaghan managed to fend them off and make a controlled forced-landing just inside the British lines. A claim for its destruction was put in for Mulzer even though the plane had not fallen into German hands. The documents that follow, uncovered by aviation historian Reinhard Kastner, demonstrate how serious a matter the recognition of such claims was to the pilots and their superiors. The day after Mulzer and Oesterreicher's team effort, a commission headed by *Maj.* Friedrich Stempel awarded Mulzer a victory for his prior 30 March claim (see above). This in turn caused Mulzer's CO, *Hptm.* Hermann Kastner, to lobby *Stofl.* 6 on Mulzer's behalf: "After the commission's decision in Cambrai on 27 April, that *Lt.* Mulzer shared in half of the air combat [victory] on 30 March, *Lt.* Mulzer has thereby shot down four enemy airmen as follows: (1) on 13 March with *Lt.* Immelmann near Serre, east of Bapaume, (2) on 30 March with two Fokkers from *FFA* 32 near Bapaume, (3) on 23 April with *Lt.* Immelmann near Monchy, (4) on 26

Above: An *Ehrenbecher* ("Honor Goblet") of the same type granted to Max Mulzer in March 1916. The goblet, initially made of silver and then of silver-plated iron towards the end of the war, was first distributed to airmen with several victories around the end of 1915. Thereafter, it typically went to airmen to commemorate their first victory. In Mulzer's case, however, it appears to have been more of a consolation prize that acknowledged his role in helping Max Immelmann bag his tenth victim.

April with *Lt.* Oesterreicher near Lens. I therefore request that he be mentioned in the *Bericht der Oberste Heeresleitung* (Supreme Command's Daily Report)."[12] At the time, four victories was the hurdle that fighter pilots had to be overcome before their names would appear in this nationwide publication. Evidently, Kastner believed Mulzer had achieved that goal, despite the fact that some of his successes were shared with or officially granted to others. *Feldflugchef* (Chief of Army Field Aviation) *Maj.* Hermann Thomsen reviewed Kastner's request and ruled that Mulzer's name would be submitted for mention in the *Bericht der Oberste Heeresleitung* the next time that he achieved a victory on his own.[13] In effect then, Thomsen was saying that the four actions Kastner cited only added up to three and that a fourth solo effort would be needed

Above: The Bavarian Pilot's Badge (left) was of the same overall design as the German Army Pilot's Badge (right) except that it displayed a Bavarian crown at its top instead of a Hohenzollern crown.

for Mulzer to meet the necessary requirement.

In the meantime, Mulzer received Bavaria's Pilot's Badge on 1 May. Apparently, he had never formally completed the three tests normally required to earn it. But in cases such as his, where a pilot's combat experience and record merited it, the badge was granted anyway. May also brought Mulzer Hamburg's Hanseatic Cross.

Thanks again to Reinhard Kastner's research, we now have the individual reports submitted by the three pilots involved in the events surrounding Mulzer's fourth victory. On 31 May, five FE.2b and two Martinsyde G100 aircraft from RFC No.23 Squadron were spotted near Cambrai. Mulzer himself wrote: "Airplane: E.IV 168/16, pilot *Lt.* Mulzer. Flight time: 10:40–12:04, weather hazy. Flight path: Douai–Arras–Cambrai–Arras–Douai. I took off in pursuit of an enemy squadron. We three Fokkers were rather close together when we suddenly saw the squadron flying east to west. Five Vickers biplanes flew in tight formation; about 500 meters above and behind them were two very quick, small, fuselaged biplanes, which dove down steeply toward the others as soon as they saw us. We attacked; there was a very lively air battle near Cambrai. The squadron did not want us to get at their backs and attacked again and again from the front. After lengthy, mutual, wild banking and circling the squadron flew off again in perfect order to the west. One fuselaged biplane was close off my right wing, the other close off my left. During the pursuit of the squadron to the west, I saw another Fokker somewhat higher than me to the right who then flew away over me. Since the enemy fliers off

my left wing were a little more widely dispersed, I tried several times to cull one out and eventually succeeded. He came under some pretty intense fire, but a Vickers and a fuselaged biplane forced me to let him go. These two latter airplanes caused me so much trouble that I could no longer concern myself with the attacked one. I pursued the squadron and made repeated, new attacks but was forced to turn around by antiaircraft fire at the Front."[14]

Uffz. Wolfgang Heinemann, one of the other Fokker pilots, reported: "Airplane: E.IV 172/16. Flight time: 10:42–12:35 (with stopover). After ascending in pursuit of an enemy squadron, I encountered it near Cambrai along with two other Fokkers from my *Abteilung*. Five enemy airplanes flew close together at 2800 meters altitude, while two combat planes were above the other five at about 3000 meters. We were just starting our attack on the squadron when the two combat planes pushed down to the five, well-formationed aircraft and protected them by starting an air battle. After initial circling over the same spot and violent shooting at one another, the squadron, holding their formation well, flew to the west. In doing this, the Vickers airplane flying off my left wing stood somewhat away from the others. At that point I attacked this airplane from above and behind and forced it further and further to the left. I noticed a Fokker under me to the left who also pursued this airplane. While circling after our initial attack on the entire squadron, I lost sight of the third Fokker and did not see it again. I drew closer to the Vickers I had shot up and broke off from him only at 1500 meters altitude when I saw him going down in a great arc. Meanwhile, the squadron had disappeared. I did not know where I was and landed at Quéant airfield which was located right beneath me. The separated Vickers had landed smoothly about five kilometers away near Inchy [-en-Artois]. After adding to my gasoline supply, I flew back to Douai." Heinemann also wrote a more lengthy (and dramatic) account of the fight for a magazine. Some excerpts: "...the two small, fast, English fighter planes protected the remaining five airplanes in the squadron which were flying in tight, perfect formation. These beautiful, snow-white little things protected the five, slow, remaining machines from our attack, flying from one to the other like an anxious mother. Then we attacked – only for a few seconds each time – but repeatedly and inexorably. But because the Englishmen always flew in perfect formation – quite an aeronautical achievement during constant twisting and turning – we could never separate one out from the others; for only then could we have dealt with it. So whenever we attacked one, the entire squadron always gathered

Above: This grainy image was presented on a postcard whose sales proceeds went to buy Christmas gifts for Brunswick servicemen in 1916. It shows the Duke of Brunswick, Ernst August (facing toward the camera, fifth from right), just after he had presented his duchy's War Merit Cross to *Uffz*. Wolfgang Heinemann (center, walking away). Max Mulzer (fifth from left wearing his white-banded 8th *Chevauleger-Regiment* service cap) and *Oblt*. Max Immelmann (far left) also attended the ceremony.

around us and we Fokkers had to leave the scene immediately. I remember quite clearly, for example, how I finally had a biplane quite close in front of me – in the next instant I was above him and could no longer shoot – and how I looked around and suddenly saw four other opponents under my tail furiously firing at me! I pulled up straightaway and removed myself from further attacks. In the next moment another opponent came before my gun sight and I fired again until I lost him in all the twisting and turning and found another. We buzzed around, mixed it up and went after each other in this manner for 15 minutes (which seems like an eternity, considering that the usual air combat takes only a few seconds!) ...suddenly I saw an Englishman fire off a red flare and the Englishmen immediately broke off the air engagement and pulled away toward the west, still (damn it all!) in tight formation. I looked around our former battlefield for a moment. I only saw one Fokker under me, the third had disappeared. Was he shot down? There was no time for further consideration because I was alive, flying and everything was OK with me and my machine. This meant: be relentless and keep on fighting!

Indeed, now that the enemies had departed to the west, we Fokkers had our best chance. In most cases, our opponents' machines could only fire forward.[15] If we now attacked the Englishmen from behind, there was not much they could do about it... then I noticed that one machine to the left, i.e., on the south side of the English formation, had somewhat moved away from the other six. I immediately attacked him laterally from the right with another Fokker underneath me in support. Hurrah! The machine separated even further from the others, it dove madly, I did too... and I shot, shot and shot. Well, I will never forget the sight: the dark brown creature with blue-and-white cockades in the middle of its wings. I could sense it; the opponent became unsteady, timorous, uncertain – and at 1500 meters height it finally went down in a great arc toward the ground, deeper and deeper...then it disappeared."[16]

The third Fokker pilot was none other than Max Immelmann, who had his own harrowing tale to tell: "Airplane: E.IV 127/15. Flight time: 10:50–11:30 in the afternoon. I immediately took off after receiving a message that six to eight English aircaft were on the way from Monchy to Cambrai. When I sighted the squadron, I shot off a flare in order to make *Lt.* Mulzer and *Uffz.* Heinemann aware of the squadron. The enemy squadron flew in formation at about 2500 meters altitude. Inexplicably, two protective airplanes immediately flew down to the squadron's altitude.[17] I fired at one of the two but without any apparent success. I turned to an FE biplane that flew furthest to the left. I opened fire at 300 meters and drew nearer, constantly firing at so small a distance that I thought I would collide with him. The enemy immediately went down in a gliding, spiral flight. I observed that he landed south of the Cambrai–Arras road. I cannot judge whether another Fokker was involved in the fight; both of the other Fokkers were higher than me, one about 50 meters and the other about 150 meters above and behind me. After I saw that the enemy had been done in, I turned to an English fighter plane. Suddenly, half of my propeller broke off from a propeller shot, the motor broke from its mount, and the airplane hung down and spun around several times over the right wing. I got control of the airplane again after a fall of about 1200 meters, stopped the engine and landed smoothly near Sauchy-Lestrée. I do not know to what extent another Fokker participated. On my apparatus are traces of hits on the engine cowling and an enemy projectile appears to have pierced a brace on the engine mount."[18]

Then we have the account of Capt. Harold Wyllie (the English flight leader): "When over Marquion, the Scouts suddenly swooped down and I knew we were attacked. I had ordered them to do this as I was well aware that they could not turn much to fight their fixed gun and hoped they would draw the enemy down on to the stern guns of the escort. I turned round after Solly [Lt. A.N. Solley, observer] and fired our drum back and he got in another one from the bow gun. I did not turn completely again after this as I realised that if we kept on turning with the wind, we should never get out. The Fokkers evidently worked on some pre-arranged plan as they were firing small white lights before swooping down. After the first attack which was made between us and the sun, the enemy showed much more caution in approaching near. It was in this first attack I think that Cairn Duff was shot down. Allen [2Lt. E.F. Allen in FE.2b 5235] had his observer (Powell) [Lt. L.C. Powell] shot dead as he was firing back and I rather think he got his man too as three of us saw one Fokker going down anyhow, side slipping and nose diving. Anyway Powell had his gun sight 'on' as the bullet grazed his trigger finger and struck him in the eye. He fell back into the nacelle breaking one of his legs in the fall. Allen was now defenceless and in spite of the fact that the machine was shot to 'bits'

just managed to scrape back over the lines, when his engine stopped. He got back into the aerodrome. While all this was going on Solly was making his notes in a most cool manner. I got him to man the after gun three times when I saw a Fokker coming up behind, but the escort kept him off."[19]

The unfortunate victim was FE.2b 6345 of RFC No.23 Squadron, which indeed set down near Inchy, south of the Cambrai–Arras road. The men who manned it, 2nd Lt. A. Cairne-Duff (pilot) and Cpl. George E Maxwell, had both been wounded and were taken into custody. Given these four accounts, it is difficult to explain today why Mulzer was given the kill. When carefully comparing them to one another, it would appear that Immelmann shot down 6345 during his initial pass as indicated by Wyllie; and Immelmann's Fokker was the one that was observed to side slip and nose dive after he had shot off his propeller. Then either Heinemann or Mulzer (or both) peppered 5235, killing its observer. Heinemann broke off but Mulzer continued fighting and pursued Wyllie's 5215 until two of Wyllie's comrades and antiaircraft fire chased Mulzer away. Perhaps Immelmann felt he owed Mulzer for the 23 April victory that Immelmann himself admitted had not really been his, and agreed to give him this one. In any event, FE.2b 6345 went down in the books as Mulzer's fourth victory, which was indeed announced in the 2 June *Bericht der Oberste Heeresleitung* as promised. Accordingly, confusion still exists today over which – or what portion – of the prior four events cited by Hermann Kastner actually counted towards Mulzer's first three official victories.

June 10th was a special day for Mulzer because he was awarded both the Iron Cross, 1st Class and Anhalt's Friedrich Cross, 2nd Class. Then on 12 June 1916, *FFA 62* was reassigned to the Eastern Front but left behind its Fokker contingent. *FFA 5b*, under the command of *Oblt.* Friedrich Moosmaier, took the departed unit's place at La Brayelle airfield and oversaw the Fokker group now designated as *Kampfeinsitzer-Kommando (KEK) 3*.

Late on 18 June, *KEK 3* took off in force to intercept a group of FE.2s from RFC No.25 Squadron. Mulzer and *Lt.* Albert Oesterreicher rose into the air first, followed by *Oblt.* Max Immelmann, *Uffz.* Wolfgang Heinemann, and *Vzfw.* Alfred Prehn. Mulzer was the first to arrive and later reported: "Around 10:00 on the evening of 18 June, I had an air combat with an English Vickers biplane northeast of Lens. The enemy airplane worked quite skillfully and tried to get me with continual machine gun fire. I constantly pursued the opponent and finally, after several turns, forced him to land, whereby I descended to about 150 meters. I went to the landing site today and was able to determine that the enemy plane had received several shots from behind that also probably wounded the pilot; furthermore, the wings displayed several bullet holes. I had fired approximately 500–600 shots during the course of the battle. The English airplane, heavily damaged by several hits, was forced to land some 100 meters south of the canal near Fourquières [-lè-Lens]."[20] This was FE.2b 4909 that pilot 2Lt. John R.B. Savage managed to land before succumbing to his wounds. Airman 2nd Class Robinson, also injured, survived and was made a prisoner.

This was the same fight in which Max Immelmann met his death.[21] It has long been asserted in other studies that 4909 was really his victory and that Mulzer had been given the credit since his dead friend could not claim it.[22] The account above, however, clearly debunks that notion and identifies the victory as Mulzer's alone.

The reason that Mulzer so carefully described the nature and direction of the bullet holes in his report is that a flak unit had also submitted a claim for the downed plane. Once again, a commission reviewed the matter and eventually awarded the victory to Mulzer later that month; but not before he had brought down his next victim on 22 June, which was immediately recognized as his fifth official success. Therefore, although FE.2b 4909 was Mulzer's fifth chronologically, it was entered into his record as his sixth.

Mulzer's fifth official victory (his chronological sixth) occurred on the morning of the same day that Immelmann's memorial service was held. Mulzer's CO, Friedrich Moosmaier, reported: "*Lt.* Mulzer of *KEK* 3 took off around 8:54 a.m. on 22 June due to fire directed at the enemy by an antiaircraft battery. He intercepted the enemy airplane north of Hulluch, cut it off on its way back to its own lines and forced it to make an emergency landing north of Hulluch in battle zone 13 between the first and second lines (Bavarian Infantry Regiment 9). The pilot is severely wounded, the observer unwounded and taken prisoner. *Lt.* Mulzer landed about 10:12 a.m. There were two machine guns in the airplane. The airplane was salvaged by *Feldflieger-Abteilung* 2b. No one but *Lt.* Mulzer participated in the air combat. This *Abteilung* requests that the shot-down plane be counted as *Lt.* Mulzer's sixth."[23] The aircraft, FE.2b 5209, belonged to RFC No.25 Squadron – the same unit that Immelmann had been fighting when he had been killed four days earlier. Its seriously wounded pilot, 2Lt. J.L.P. Armstrong, died soon after his observer, Sgt. G. Topliffe, had been taken into custody.

Above: This group photo of Mulzer and members of *FFA* 5b was taken on the steps of their officer's mess shortly after Mulzer's *Pour le Mérite* investiture. In the front row (left to right): *Oblt.* Pfleger, Mulzer, *Oblt.* Friedrich Moosmaier (CO), *Lt.* Offermann. Behind them, beginning with the two men in the background behind the shrubbery at far left: *Dr.* Kalkbrenner, *Lt.* C. Schroder, *Lt.* E. Schroeder, *Lt.* Geys, *Lt.* Gerstle, *Lt.* Rietzler, *Oblt.* von Kitzing, *Lt.* Köchel, *Lt.* Albert Oesterreicher (below Köchel), *Lt.* Ungewitter, *Lt.* Kolb, *Oblt.* Fillisch, *Oblt.* Schroeder.

Mulzer may have felt a certain sense of satisfaction in avenging the death of his friend when he attended Immelmann's memorial service later that afternoon in the garden of Douai's War Hospital A. Chosen to carry the deceased's *Ordenskissen*, Mulzer led the procession from the hospital to the railway station where Immelmann's corpse was transported back home to Dresden for burial.[24]

Hptm. Oswald Boelcke, who had flown over from his base at Sivry-sur-Meuse to attend Immelmann's funeral ceremonies, stayed on at Douai for awhile to participate in several sorties with *KEK* 3. One of them involved "six Vickers machines over [Henin-] Lietard. I took off with the other Fokkers from Douai... I engaged one of them and set about him properly; I must have hit him because a great yellow column of smoke came out of his engine... But he escaped me and got across the lines in a glide... I could not quite finish him off because my left gun jammed when I had shot away all the ammunition in my right. Meanwhile the other Fokkers had got to grips with the Squadron. I saw another 160 H.P. machine (Lieut. Mulzer) set about an Englishman in fine style. As the latter soon received reinforcements and the other Fokkers were all busily engaged, I found I could at least give Mulzer some help by

Above: According to the notation on its back, this is a picture of Mulzer and four nurses in Douai on 24 July 1916.

Above: Mulzer stands before the camera in the courtyard of his family home in Memmingen.

taking on an Englishman and drawing him away – my opponent did not know that I could not fire a shot. Mulzer saw and recognised me and started a most cheeky attack; unfortunately, he only scored a half-victory, like the one I had got earlier on. I hung on there until I saw Mulzer fly back."[25] It seems that Boelcke was describing a battle with RFC No.25 Squadron that occurred on 26 June. Three of the unit's aircraft were shot up that day by Fokker fighters but were able to escape back to their lines. FE.2b 6346 was damaged and forced to land near Beuvry. Observer Cpl. J.H. Waller was unhurt but his pilot, 2Lt. G.R. McCubbin, was wounded in the right arm. (This was the same crew that the British claimed had downed Max Immelmann eight days before.) 2Lt. R. Sherwell, flying FE.2b 6334, returned to base with a dead observer, Airman 2nd Class H. Chadwick, who had been killed by three shots to the chest. FE.2b 5212, manned by Lt. R.C.B. Riley (pilot) and Lt. E.H. Bird, was engaged over Mazingarbe and made an emergency landing nearby during which it hit a string of barbed wire, overturned and collapsed in a heap. Riley suffered a concussion in the crash

but recovered. Bird, who had been shot in the back during the air fight and then suffered a broken wrist and dislocated shoulder in the crash, died the next day.[26] Friedrich Moosmaier's report to *Stofl.* 6 points to 5212 as Mulzer's 'probable': "On 26 June, *Lt.* Mulzer and two other Fokker airmen went up and a violent air combat with several Vickers took place over Loos, during which he was lightly wounded in the left foot by a 2 cm long fragment from an infantry shell. *Lt.* Mulzer shot down an English Vickers in this air combat that went down in a dive near Grenay les Brébis [note: Grenay is adjacent to Mazingarbe] and was wrecked. Flak bombardment did not take place. This *Abteilung* requests that the shot-down plane be counted as *Lt.* Mulzer's seventh."[27] It was not to be, however, and as Boelcke indicated in his account, no victories were awarded for their efforts, most likely because the aircraft in question did not fall into German hands.

Above: During his final home leave in late August/early September 1916, Mulzer went to Karl Müller's photography studio in Memmingen to pose for a series of portraits, two of which are shown here. In a third example presented on page 74 above, Mulzer had worn his *Grossordensschnalle* (medals bar) on his breast, which is not visible in the two below. This is because in the first, he had actually removed it. In the second, however, it was erased from the negative (note the distinct marring effect on Mulzer's tunic where the medals bar had once been), apparently because someone preferred that look.

Mulzer was transferred to *Abwehrkommando Nord (AKN)* on 1 July. There at its base near Bertincourt he joined *Lts.* Franz Diemer, Walter Dingel, Gericke, Hohberg, Gustav Leffers, Burkhard Lehmann and Schulte (Adolf?) under the oversight of *FFA* 32 and its CO, *Hptm.* Oswald Ritter. The next day, Mulzer encountered BE.2c 2654 of RFC No.9 Squadron while flying Fokker E.IV 176/16: "Around 6:00 in the evening, flying along the Front, I saw shellbursts near Bapaume. I was at 3500 meters altitude, the enemy flier, a BE, at about 2800 meters. I dove down at him and delivered some shots, whereupon he turned sharply to fly back to the west, and I gave him another 80 shots from a distance of about 50 meters. The enemy airplane suddenly caught fire, rose up once, fell, caught itself

again and descended, burning, in spirals down to about 500 meters where it then fell straight to the ground and was consumed by flames along with its occupants."[28] The hapless crewmen were Lt. I.C. MacDonnell (pilot) and 2Lt. H.A. Williamson.

By the end of June, a commission had officially accepted Mulzer's 18 June victory, giving him a confirmed total of six downed aircraft. At this point in the war, a fighter pilot with six victories was normally eligible for the Royal Hohenzollern House Order, Knight's Cross with Swords. Accordingly, Max Mulzer was recommended for the decoration and awarded it on 7 July 1916 – a few days after his seventh success. By this time, he had already returned to *FFA* 5b's *KEK* 3 Fokker contingent, so his service with *Abwehrkommando Nord* had been

Above & Left: These pictures demonstrate that Mulzer also posed with his father (on home leave as well) at Karl Müller's studio. One of Mulzer's comrades once remarked that he had referred to his father as "his best friend."

quite brief.

Lt. Eric C. Jowett (pilot) and Cpl. R. Johnstone of RFC No.4 Squadron were conducting an important photographic mission for the Somme offensive on 8 July when Mulzer emerged from the clouds and pounced on their BE.2d 5765. After expending 80–100 shots during his initial run, Mulzer pulled up and watched as the crippled plane, courageously flown by its wounded pilot, crash landed near Miraumont. Johnstone was taken prisoner and Jowett died the next day. This all-important eighth victory secured the *Pour le Mérite* for Mulzer,

Above & Left: Two snapshots taken during Mulzer's investiture with the Military Max-Joseph Order in September 1916 at La Brayelle airfield. In the first, he stands at attention before *GenMaj*. Paul *Ritter* von Köberle, who is holding the decoration in his hand at left. In the second, Köberle is stepping back after having just affixed the medal to a buttonhole in Mulzer's tunic.

which was given to him as of that day. He was the first Bavarian airman and only the sixth Bavarian soldier to be so honored. *Oblt.* Arthur Pfleger, an observer with *FFA* 5b, recalled: "One day we were delighted by the award of the *Pour le Mérite* to *Lt.* Mulzer. The solemn presentation of the high honor took place in the morning. In triumph, we led our young comrade, who was loved and admired by all, to the officer's mess in order to throw him a party befitting the occasion. Since the afternoon alone was insufficient, we took the evening and half the night to do so."[29] Mulzer's hometown of Memmingen celebrated too. On 9 July, Town Councilman Hugo Besemfelder issued the following resolutions: "(1) that today flags bedeck the town hall for 24 hours in honor of *Lt.* Max Mulzer, (2) that a street – the best candidate being Reichshainstrasse, where his parents' house stands and where he spent his youth – be renamed 'Mulzerstrasse,' (3) that he be

informed of these resolutions through an artistically executed salutory address and the address be solemnly delivered to him after completion, (4) that the honored one and perhaps his father (currently a Surgeon-Major 2nd Class) both be informed in the field of these resolutions by their city colleagues, and the newspapers immediately notified of this."[30] Famed artist Max Unold created the salutory address document and "Reichshainstrasse" was indeed changed to "Mulzerstrasse" (though today it is known as "Mulzergraben").

July 21st brought the sobering news of the losses of two of Mulzer's colleagues. *Lt.* Otto Parschau, who had been in command of *Abwehrkommando Nord* for only one week, had been severely wounded in a fight with RFC No.24 Squadron over Grévillers, had crash-landed and then succumbed to his injuries.[31] Mulzer's squadron mate, Wolfgang Heinemann, was also killed over Harcourt during a scrap that pitted at least four *KEK* 3 Fokkers against a combined force of BE.2s from RFC No.12 Squadron and FE.2s from No.23 Squadron. Mulzer, who had learned of the honors accorded him by his hometown, probably had Parschau and Heinemann

Above: An informal group photo of the men attending the party thrown for Max *Ritter* von Mulzer following his investiture with the Military Max-Joseph Order. Seated in the foreground (left to right): Ranft, *Lt.* Geys, Scheuring, *Oblt.* Friedrich Moosmaier (CO), Zimmer-Vorhaus, *Lt.* Constantin Krefft, *Lt.* Weber. Seated behind the table: *Oblt.* Fillisch, *GenMaj.* Paul *Ritter* von Köberle, Mulzer, *Gen.* Oskar *Ritter und Edler* von Xylander, unknown, Heinemann (not Wolfgang). Back row, standing: *Lt.* Köchel, unknown, *Lt.* Ungewitter, *Lt.* C. Schröder, Seibert, Fleischmann, Ledermann, Joens, *Dr.* Kalkbrenner. (photo courtesy of Reinhard Kastner)

in his thoughts when he responded in an open letter to the citizens of Memmingen on 29 July: "Permit me to express my most cordial thanks for the great honors you unanimously approved for me. I am extremely proud to be allowed to contribute in a small way to the glory of our long-famous free-city. And yet a shameful feeling has gradually enveloped me that perhaps too much honor has been given to me, because I still have not done more than all the brave sons of the city who have gone off to defend the Fatherland and given much more, indeed everything, in having to sacrifice their lives, while the fortunes of war have smiled upon me so extraordinarily. It is my ardent wish, and I will continue to strive with all my strength, to pay this debt of thanks back in service to the country and to do credit to Memmingen. With my entire heart, I wish rich blessings always to the city that has been my home and to all its children. With the greatest respect and gratitude, *Leutnant* Max Mulzer."[32]

Confusion surrounds Mulzer's final two

successes, just as it did with his earliest victories. Several modern sources relate that he was credited with his ninth victim near Hulluch on 22 July, but there are no corresponding British losses to fit that scenario. In fact, because of the day's bad weather conditions, only two British planes were listed as having been in any kind of fight. Both incidents occurred much further south near Albert and the planes returned safely. Thus the identity of Mulzer's

Facing Page: Four scenes from Mulzer's memorial service in Douai. The first shows his coffin, with *Ordenskissen* placed before it, lying in state in War Hospital A's courtyard. The second has *Oblt.* Friedrich Moosmaier delivering his eulogy to the attendees. The third captures Mulzer's coffin being carried out of the courtyard, led by *Lt.* Constantin Krefft with Mulzer's *Ordenskissen*. Last, we see the gun carriage bearing Mulzer's remains as it wends its way through Douai's streets to the train station. Krefft is behind the gun carriage, *Dr.* Max Mulzer (wearing spiked helmet) is two men behind Krefft and Moosmaier is at far right.

Above & Facing Page: Three scenes from Mulzer's funeral in Memmingen. In the first, Father Rippler presides over the Catholic services held in the city mortuary's courtyard. Mulzer's father (in spiked helmet) can be seen in the left archway standing beneath the wingtip of the Pfalz Parasol that had been specially placed there. The second has *Dr.* Mulzer, flanked by his sons Albert (left) and Josef (right), trailing immediately behind the casket as it heads toward the cemetery. Krefft accompanies them a little to the right. The final photo shows Mulzer's remains being lowered into their final resting place.

ninth, if it indeed occurred on 22 July, remains a mystery. Mulzer's service record, however, states that his ninth fell on 3 August – a victory that most modern sources list as his tenth. In this action he met up with FE.2b 4272 of *KEK* 3's old nemesis, RFC No.25 Squadron, and shot it down in flames near Sallaumines/Lens. Sapper E.M. des Brisay (observer) was found dead in the wreck and his pilot, 2Lt. Kenneth Mathewson, died within hours in a German hospital. In Mulzer's service record and the 6th Army's list of downed enemy aircraft, his tenth is said to have occurred on 9 August, when he shot down FE.2b 6996 of RFC No.25 Squadron. It too crashed in flames near La Coulotte (near Avion). Mulzer gave this report: "Around 7:30 in the evening I noticed a Vickers biplane circling over Lens that was being fired upon by our antiaircraft guns in the vicinity of Acheville. When I reached him, he flew off toward the west. I delivered about 80–100 shots at very close range, after which a smoke cloud rose from his engine. He sought to escape by flying in banking circles toward the west. I again delivered about 100 shots, whereupon he, in a steep banking glide, crashed north of Sallaumines and overturned. The other Vickers apparatus was shot down at night

by our infantry and landed in the barbed wire at our front lines."[33] Obviously, he believed this was a victory and it was listed as such in his service record, which therefore appears to be reliable. Accordingly, the alleged victory near Hulluch on 22 July is questionable and either might never have occurred or was never confirmed.

Mulzer achieved another first for Bavarian airmen when he was awarded that kingdom's highest military decoration, the Military Max-Joseph Order, Knight's Cross, which entitled him to carry the non-hereditary title of nobility, *"Ritter* von" ("Knight"). Though the award was granted on 21 August, it was backdated to 8 July – the date he had been bestowed with Prussia's *Orden Pour le Mérite*. Shortly afterwards, and before the high honor could be physically conferred upon him, Mulzer and his father (who had been awarded the Iron Cross 1st Class in recognition of his medical services) both went home on leave to Memmingen. Mulzer returned to the Front in September, where he finally received his Military Max-Joseph Order at the hands of *GenMaj.* Paul *Ritter* von Köberle at *FFA* 5b's La Brayelle airfield outside of Douai.[34]

Mulzer was not in much of a mood to celebrate,

however. He had seen too many colleagues die since the summer; and after he learned of fellow *Pour le Mérite* recipient Kurt Wintgens' death on 25 September, he adopted a fatalistic attitude. One of his *FFA* 5b squadron mates, identified only as "*Oberleutnant* F.," related: "Yes, the summer of 1916 was a very sad time at Douai. It began on 18 June with Immelmann!... On 21 July, our little Heinemann fell in air combat, on 12 August our

Kopp, on 14 September our *Lt*. Gerstle (my former pilot, who had become a Fokker pilot at the end of August), on 22 September *Oblt*. Albert (who was shot down right before our eyes)... At the dining table – [Mulzer] was sitting directly opposite me – he said: 'Now I should buy a beautiful, broad ribbon for my Max-Joseph-Knight's Order, because that will ensure that I will have a beautiful *Ordenskissen*...' In the afternoon, as he was driving away with two

comrades in a car, he said: 'I'm next. Immelmann is dead. Parschau is dead, yesterday Wintgens... now I'm next in line!' At 7:00 that evening he was dead."[35] Mulzer had gone to *Armee-Flug-Park* 6 at Valenciennes to try out a new airplane. An official report stated: *"Lt.* von Mulzer came to the depot on 26 September to fetch a newly-arrived Albatros single-seater. After final assembly, thorough inspection and a test flight by *Vzfw.* Baierlein that found it completely in order, the Albatros D.I 424/16 machine, intended for *KEK* 3 of FFA 5b, was handed over to *Lt.* von Mulzer. *Lt.* von Mulzer took off on a test flight. At about 500 meters altitude, he switched off the engine and went into a righthand turn that started off flat but then grew ever steeper and tighter until the machine hit the ground at great speed, cartwheeling over its wings. *Lt.* von Mulzer suffered a skull fracture that was instantly fatal when he struck the machine gun mount. Though the machine was destroyed, the fuselage – particularly in front of the cockpit – was practically intact, so that all the flight controls could be examined and were found completely in order. Eyewitness accounts of the crash and the examination of the machine provide no information whatsoever as to the cause of the crash."[36]

FFA 5b wired a brief message to Memmingen: *"Lt.* Mulzer crashed fatally this evening. Please inform his mother of this gently."[37]

Max *Ritter* von Mulzer's coffin was placed in the garden of Douai's War Hospital A at the same spot where Max Immelmann's had lain just three months earlier. On 1 October, Army chaplain Stadler presided over a brief memorial ceremony, during which Crown Prince Wilhelm's representative and *Oblt.* Friedrich Moosmaier delivered eulogies. Then the coffin, surrounded by numerous wreaths and floral tributes, was lifted onto the shoulders of an honor guard and led outside by *Lt.* Constantin Krefft, who carried the deceased's *Ordenskissen.* It was placed on a gun carriage and the long line of men in attendance, headed by Krefft, Max Mulzer's father and parson Stadler, followed it through the streets of Douai to the train station. One eyewitness wrote: "Many soldiers looked on, many local citizens too. They kept quiet and observed the spectacle with curiosity. The procession filed past the command building and the airmen's mess, where he had spent so many merry hours... An officer, plain in appearance, inconspicuously and modestly joined the procession along the way; I knew the face but could not place him. A wagon filled with beautiful flowers and boughs that had been arranged like an artful painting was at the station. It would take him back to the homeland. The chaplain gave a benediction.

Three honor salvos cracked thunderously. Hands went to service caps: the final salute of his comrades in the field. And the music played: 'I Had a Comrade.' The ceremony was over. Then the same officer stepped up to the casket and laid down a small wreath. Now I knew him – it was Boelcke."[38]

Mulzer's casket was transported to Memmingen, where it was placed under an honor guard in the city mortuary's courtyard in front of a Pfalz Parasol airplane. The guards were comprised of NCO airmen and soldiers from a local *Pioneer batallion.* Father Rippler, the city's parish priest, began Mulzer's funeral ceremony at 4:30 p.m. on 3 October. Almost all the town's dignitaries and citizens attended, as well as numerous military representatives of the Bavarian armed forces, the Air Service and the various units Mulzer had served with. Mulzer's family then led a procession from the mortuary to the cemetery, where two airplanes laden with flowers circled overhead. Like the services performed in Douai, a final blessing, three gunfire salutes and the strains of *"Ich hatt' ein Kameraden"* ended the proceedings.

Endnotes

[1] Schobachter, *"Unser Allgäuer Fliegerheld,"* p.1.
[2] Schobachter, *"Unser Allgäuer Fliegerheld,"* p.2.
[3] Reinhard Kastner (*"Leutnant* Max *Ritter* von Mulzer," p.610) informs us that on 4 November 1915, *Abwehrkommandos* I and II (essentially aircraft protection units) were formed under *FFA* 62's jurisdiction. *Abwehrkommando* II was originally comprised of *Leutnante* Max Immelmann, Albert Oesterreicher, Ernst Hess and Alfred Prehn. Then on 7 February 1916, three *Kampfeinsitzer-Kommando* units were formed and attached to each of the 6th Army's reconnaissance groups. The former *Abwehrkommando* II became *KEK* 3 and remained under *FFA* 62's jurisdiction.
[4] *Eagle of Lille,* p.178; *Adler von Lille,* p.152.
[5] *Eagle of Lille,* p.174; *Adler von Lille,* p.155.
[6] We are indebted to the excellent research conducted by Reinhard Kastner (*"Leutnant* Max *Ritter* von Mulzer") for this report and several others that follow.
[7] Ibid.
[8] Sieverts, *"Ein Tag bei meiner alten Feldfliegerabteilung im Westen,"* p.16–17.
[9] *Eagle of Lille,* p.192; *Adler von Lille,* p.166. "Monchy" in this case was Monchy-le-Preux.
[10] Immelmann. *Meine Kampfflüge,* p.120.
[11] Oesterreicher was among Germany's earliest pilots, having received Pilot's License No.515 on 15 September 1913. He survived almost the entire war only to be killed on 8 November 1918 in a flying accident at Bavarian Military Flying School 5 at Gersthofen.

[12] Document: *Chef des Flugwesens* Br.10369 Fl. St.O.Fl.6 No.9857, dated 28.4.1916.

[13] Document: *Chef des Flugwesens* No.15427, dated 2.5.1916.

[14] For this combat report and the two that follow, see Kastner, "*Leutnant* Max *Ritter* von Mulzer," pp.615–16.

[15] That is, the observer's flexible gun was mounted on the nose of the FE.2.

[16] Heinemann, "*Mit Immelmann und Mulzer in der Luftschlacht zusammen,*"pp.480–82.

[17] Evidently, Immelmann felt the two Martinsydes should have delayed their move until a later time when they could have used the advantage of their increased diving speed to attack the Fokkers.

[18] Franz Immelmann later wrote that his brother actually shot himself down due to a failure of his machine gun interruptor mechanism. See *Eagle of Lille*, pp.200–03; *Adler von Lille*, pp.173–75.

[19] Hart, *Somme Success*, pp.43–45.

[20] See Kastner, "*Leutnant* Max *Ritter* von Mulzer," pp.617–19.

[21] See Volume 1 of this series, pp.77–80.

[22] There are several reasons for this. First, some German newspapers printed exaggerated accounts of Immelmann's last stand that said that he had downed two (or more) aircraft before his death. Second, the two British airmen who engaged Immelmann just before his plane broke up in midair testified that he had been pursuing 4909. He may well have been, but this does not necessarily exclude Mulzer and they may not have seen him.

[23] See Kastner, "*Leutnant* Max *Ritter* von Mulzer," p.620.

[24] See Volume 1 of this series, pp.81–83.

[25] Werner, *Knight of Germany*, p.179; *Boelcke: der Mensch*, p.164.

[26] See Lawson, "Maximilian von Mulzer, The Green Knight" p.154.

[27] See Kastner, "*Leutnant* Max *Ritter* von Mulzer," pp.621–22.

[28] See Kastner, "*Leutnant* Max *Ritter* von Mulzer," p.622.

[29] Ibid.

[30] Document possessed by Stadtarchiv Memmingen.

[31] Parschau, whom Mulzer had recently served with at *Abwehrkommando Nord*, had earned his *Pour le Mérite* on 10 July, only two days after Mulzer. *Lt.* Werner Schramm, another *AKN* Fokker pilot, was shot down during the same engagement.

[32] Document possessed by Stadtarchiv Memmingen.

[33] *Flugsport* 3 (1917), p.71.

[34] Some sources give the ceremony's date as 6 September while others list it as 19 September.

[35] Heinemann was killed in a fight over Harcourt with

Above: According to the handwritten caption on the back of this photo of Mulzer, this was "the usual situation at the airdrome when there was no flying."

BE.2s from RFC No.12 Squadron and FE.2s from No.23 Squadron. *Lt.* Hans Kopp, another Fokker pilot, met his end over Sallaumines before the gun of a Martinsyde G100 flown by Lt. P.A. Wright of No.27 Squadron. *Lt.* Franz Gerstle was shot down near Rancourt (probably during a fight with BE.12s from No.19 Squadron) and *Oblt.* Karl Albert was bested in combat by Capt. D.O. Mulholland in No.40 Squadron's FE.8 6384.

Mulzer's reference to needing a large display ribbon for his Military Max-Joseph Order probably stems from the fact that during the war a recipient normally wore it on a small ribbon suspended from one of his tunic's buttonholes.

[36] See Kastner, "*Leutnant* Max *Ritter* von Mulzer," p.626. Though this is purely speculative, "*Oberleutnant* F." might have been the *Oblt.* Fillisch who appeared in several *FFA* 5b photos with Mulzer.

[37] Document possessed by Stadtarchiv Memmingen.

[38] See Schobachter, "*Unser Allgäuer Fliegerheld,*" p.6.

Mulzer – The Aircraft

Not much information has survived regarding the aircraft flown by Max *Ritter* von Mulzer, and photos of them are unfortunately quite rare.

LVG B.II
(Late August–November 1915)

Mulzer went to *Flieger-Ersatz-Abteilung* 1b at Schleissheim for pilot training on 20 August 1915 and completed his course there in November. M1 tells us that at least one of the planes he trained on was an LVG B.II.

Pfalz E.II 226/15
(Late January 1916–?)

M2, a photo capturing Mulzer in a Pfalz E.II fighter, appeared in Reinhard Kastner's article on Mulzer. There it was stated that the serial number was 226/15 (it is barely visible in small print just behind the cockpit at the top of the side of the fuselage) and that Mulzer flew it when he was with *FFA* 62. In that case, this E.II was probably used by Mulzer during his early time with the unit since we know that he flew Fokker fighters from March 1916 forward. Interestingly, 226/15 was the first E.II to be shipped from the Pfalz factory (probably in late November or December 1915) and may have been sent to *FFA* 62 for assessment because of the unit's experienced, successful fighter pilots (e.g., Oswald Boelcke and Max Immelmann). Mulzer was posted to *FFA* 62 in January 1916 and may have been assigned the Pfalz E.II – which by this point had already been deemed inferior to the Fokker monoplanes – because of his beginner status.

M1: *Lt.* Max Mulzer (with crash helmet looped in his left arm) poses in front of an LVG B.II during his pilot training days at Schleissheim.

M2: Mulzer sits in the cockpit of Pfalz E.II 226/15.

M3

M3: A brand new Pfalz E.II 226/15 – the first of its kind to be placed into service – sits on the factory's field. A Pfalz E.I (which sported double wing cables and an 80 hp, 7-cylinder engine versus the EII's triple cables and 100 hp, 9-cylinder engine) rests in the background. The Pfalz E.I was a license-built Morane-Saulnier H armed with a synchronized gun.

M4: A Fokker *Eindecker* flies cover over a Roland C.II *Walfisch*. Some sources have identified the *Eindecker's* pilot as Max Immelmann. Yet the back of this original photograph states in handwritten German: "Combat pilot Mulzer in the Fokker. Below him in the *Walfisch, Oblt.* Cossel and *Offz-Stv.* Windisch, the famous crew mentioned in the *Heeresbericht.*" This appears to have been a wartime identification because the reference to Windisch as an *Offizier-Stellvertreter* points to it having been recorded prior to Windisch's promotion to *Leutnant* on 5 December 1916. If the caption is accurate, this may be the only surviving photo of Max Mulzer in a Fokker *Eindecker* prior to August 1916 (see below). Windisch joined *FFA* 62 on 1 May and departed with the unit to the Eastern Front on 12 June, so the photo would have originated during that period.

M4

Fokker E-type, Fokker E.IV 168/16 (March–June 1916)

Max Immelmann referred to Mulzer as "another Fokker pilot" when he described their joint action of 13 March, so we know Mulzer was piloting a Fokker *Eindecker* by this time. However, we do not know what model(s) until Mulzer's 31 May combat report, in which he noted Fokker E.IV 168/16 as his mount. According to Fokker's E.IV acceptance records, 168/16 was most likely delivered to *FFA* 62 in April 1916, and Mulzer may have taken it over then. Subsequent, surviving reports disclose that he continued to use an E.IV due to their references to two machine guns (Fokker models E.I–III carried only one) or a 160 hp engine (distinct to the E.IV model), but they do not specify a serial number.

Fokker E.IV 176/16 (Early July 1916)

During his brief stint with *Abwehrkommando Nord* that began on 1 July, Mulzer recorded that he flew Fokker E.IV 176/16 on 2 July. Mulzer returned to *FFA* 5b's *KEK* 3 about one week later.

Fokker E.IV?, Halberstadt D.II/III?, Fokker D.I (6 July–September 1916?)

Following his return to *KEK* 3 around 6 July, Mulzer probably went back to flying a Fokker E.IV; and it is likely that this was the type of aircraft he used to down his eighth victim on 8 July, thereby earning the *Pour le Mérite*. Though he may have continued using an E.IV for some time after this, it is also possible that he switched over to the Halberstadt D.II/III fighter, which began to reach the Front in late June and grew to an operational total of 25 by the end of August. It has been reported that right before *KEK* 3 was reorganized into *Jasta* 10 on 28 September 1916, it was comprised of "a mix of Fokker monoplanes and biplanes, one Halberstadt D.II and two Albatros D.II fighters."[1] M8 informs us that Mulzer flew at least once in a Fokker D.I after it had begun arriving at the Front in August, so it is equally possible that he tried out a Halberstadt D.II/III as well. Having said this, little solid evidence exists to definitively tell us what kind of plane(s) he flew during this period.

M5–6: Two photos of the business end of a later model Fokker E.IV. Max Mulzer's 168/16 would have been quite similar in appearance with standard markings and color scheme.

M5

M7: Fokker E.IV 174/16 warms up its engine at a German airfield. Max Mulzer's 176/16, which he flew for only a very brief period, probably looked quite similar to the plane seen here except for the uncovered wheels (the E.IV's spoke wheels were normally covered with fabric).

M8

M8: *Lt.* Max Mulzer sits in the cockpit of a Fokker D.I biplane. Note the pulley mechanism (just below the upper wing in front of him) that was part of the plane's wing-warping controls.

Fokker E.I
(August 1916)

The next photo, M9, is of an early Fokker E.I that was taken at *FFA* 2b's airfield at Phalempin in August 1916 (according to a handwritten note on the reverse). The occasion was a visit by Max Mulzer, who can be seen sitting in the plane's cockpit. It is unlikely that Mulzer would have been flying such an outdated model in combat in August, so he probably used it for transport behind the lines. An album that once belonged to *FFA* 2b's *Lt.* Johann Czermak contains another image of this E.I (taken at the same time as M9) and several pictures of Mulzer. This and the fact that Phalempin is only 10 miles north of Douai indicate that Mulzer may have visited his fellow Bavarians' unit several times.

Albatros D.I 424/16
(26 September 1916)

Max *Ritter* von Mulzer crashed to his death while test flying Albatros D.I 424/16 at Valenciennes on 26 September 1916. 424/16 was only the third D.I to roll off the production line and it is a testament to his status in the Air Service that he was slated to receive one of the earliest machines.[2]

Endnotes

[1] Grosz, *Halberstadt Fighters*, p.6.
[2] The Air Service's procurement group, *Inspektion der Fliegertruppe (Idflieg)*, ordered 50 of the type with serial numbers 422 through 471.

M10–13: Four scenes taken at the crash site of Mulzer's D.I 424/16. The first photo clearly displays the tubular steel machine gun mount against which Mulzer fractured his skull upon impact.

M9: A photograph of a Fokker E.I that Mulzer flew during a visit in August 1916 to *FFA* 2b's base at Phalempin.

Mulzer – Military Service

Significant Dates

9 Jul 1893	born in Kimratshofen
1908	entered Cadet Corps
10 Jul 1914	*Fähnrich* with Bavaria's *Chevaulegers-Regiment* Nr.8
13 Dec 1914	promoted to *Leutnant*
20 Aug 1915	assigned to *Flieger-Ersatz-Abteilung* 1b
Nov 1915	assigned to *Armee-Flug-Park* 6
13 Dec 1915	assigned to *Feldflieger-Abteilung* 4b
Jan 1916	assigned to *Abwehrkommando* II (attached to *FFA* 62)
13 Mar 1916	first partial victory?
30 Mar 1916	first official victory
12 Jun 1916	assigned to *Kampfeinsitzer-Kommando* 3 (attached to *FFA* 5b)
1 Jul 1916	assigned to *Abwehrkommando Nord*
mid-Jul 1916	returned to *Kampfeinsitzer-Kommando* 3 (attached to *FFA* 5b)
8 Jul 1916	awarded *Pour le Mérite*
3 or 9 Aug 1916	final victory (#10)
26 Sep 1916	killed in flying accident
3 Oct 1916	buried in Memmingen

Service Units

10 Jul 1914–19 Aug 1915	*Chevaulegers-Regiment* Nr.8
20 Aug–Nov 1915	*Flieger-Ersatz-Abteilung* 1b
Nov–12 Dec 1915	*Armee-Flug-Park* 6
13 Dec 1915–Jan 1916	*Feldflieger-Abteilung* 4b
Jan–11 Jun 1916	*Abwehrkommando* II (attached to *FFA* 62)
12–30 Jun 1916	*Kampfeinsitzer-Kommando* 3 (attached to *FFA* 5b)
1–mid-Jul 1916	*Abwehrkommando Nord*
mid-Jul–26 Sep 1916	*Kampfeinsitzer-Kommando* 3 (attached to *FFA* 5b)

Awards

10 Oct 1914	Iron Cross, 2nd Class – Prussia
13 Mar 1916	*Ehrenbecher* – Germany
17 Apr 1916	Military Merit Order, 4th Class with Swords – Bavaria
1 May 1916	Pilot's Badge – Bavaria
? May 1916	Hanseatic Cross – Hamburg
10 Jun 1916	Friedrich Cross, 2nd Class – Anhalt
10 Jun 1916	Iron Cross, 1st Class – Prussia
7 Jul 1916	Royal Hohenzollern House Order, Knight's Cross with Swords – Prussia
8 Jul 1916	*Pour le Mérite* – Prussia
21 Aug 1916	Military Max-Joseph Order, Knight's Cross – Bavaria*

*backdated to 8 Jul 1916

Below Left: *Lt.* Max *Ritter* von Mulzer strikes a formal pose for the camera.

Below: Max *Ritter* von Mulzer's funeral in Memmingen.

Mulzer – Victory List

No.	Date	Aircraft	Location, Unit & Crew*
?	13 Mar 1916	Bristol C Scout 4678	near Serre – RFC 4: Maj. Victor A Barrington-Kennett (KIA)
1	30 Mar	BE.2c 2605	near Monchy-au-Bois – RFC 8: Lt. TC Wilson (POW), A1c. A Walker (KIA)
?	23 Apr	Vickers FB.5 5079	Monchy-le-Preux – RFC 11: 2Lt. William C Mortimer-Phelan, 2Lt. William A Scott-Brown (b-POW)
?	26 Apr	FE.2b 5232	near Souchez – RFC 18: 2Lt. JC Callaghan, 2Lt. J Mitchell (WIA) (b-made it back to British lines)
4	31 May	FE.2b 6345	near Inchy – RFC 23: 2Lt. A Cairne-Duff, Cpl. GE Maxwell (b-WIA/POW)
5	18 Jun	FE.2d 4909	near Fourquières-lè-Lens– RFC 25: 2Lt. JRB Savage (KIA), A2c. Robinson (WIA/POW)
6	22 Jun	FE.2b 5209	north of Hulluch – RFC 25: 2Lt. JLP Armstrong (KIA), Sgt. G Topliffe (POW)
7	2 Jul	BE.2c 2654	near Bapaume – RFC 9: Lt. IC MacDonnell, 2Lt. HA Williamson (b-KIA)
8	8 Jul	BE.2d 5765	near Miraumont – RFC 4: Lt. EC Jowett (DOW), Cpl. R Johnstone (POW)
?	22 Jul	?	near Hulluch – ?
9	3 Aug	FE.2b 4272	near Sallaumines – RFC 25: 2Lt. K Matthewson (DOW), Sapr. EM desBrisay (KIA)
10	9 Aug	FE.2b 6996	near La Coulotte – RFC 25: Lt CJ Hart, Lt. IA Mann (b-KIA)

*pilot listed first
b-   both occupants
DOW died of wounds
KIA   killed in action
POW prisoner of war
WIA   wounded in action

Above: Max *Ritter* von Mulzer's funeral in Memmingen.

Pour le Mérite Winners by Date of Award

Recipient	Date of Award	Recipient	Date of Award
Hptm. Oswald Boelcke	January 12, 1916	*Hptm.* Bruno Loerzer	February 12, 1918
Oblt. Max Immelmann	January 12, 1916	*Lt.* Heinrich Kroll	March 29, 1918
Oblt. Hans-Joachim Buddecke	April 14, 1916	*Kptlt.* Horst *Freiherr* Treusch von Buttlar-Brandenfels	April 9, 1918
Lt. Kurt Wintgens	July 1, 1916		
Lt. Max *Ritter* von Mulzer	July 8, 1916	*Oblt.* Ernst Udet	April 9, 1918
Lt. Otto Parschau	July 10, 1916	*Lt.* Carl Menckhoff	April 23, 1918
Lt. Walter Höhndorf	July 20, 1916	*Hptm.* Hermann Köhl	May 21, 1918
Oblt. Ernst *Freiherr* von Althaus	July 21, 1916	*Oblt.* Erich Löwenhardt	May 31, 1918
Lt. Wilhelm Frankl	August 12, 1916	*Lt.* Fritz Pütter	May 31, 1918
Hptm. Rudolf Berthold	October 12, 1916	*Oblt.* Hermann Göring	June 2, 1918
Lt. Gustav Leffers	November 5, 1916	*Lt.* Friedrich Nielebock	June 2, 1918
Lt. Albert Dossenbach	November 11, 1916	*Lt.* Rudolf Windisch	June 6, 1918
Oblt. Hans Berr	December 4, 1916	*Lt.* Wilhelm Paul Schreiber	June 8, 1918
Rittm. Manfred *Freiherr* von Richthofen	January 12, 1917	*Lt.* Hans Kirschstein	June 24, 1918
		Oblt. Otto Kissenberth	June 30, 1918
Genlt. Ernst von Hoeppner	April 8, 1917	*Lt.* Emil Thuy	June 30, 1918
Oberst Hermann von der Lieth-Thomsen	April 8, 1917	*Lt.* Peter Rieper	July 7, 1918
Lt. Werner Voss	April 8, 1917	*Lt.* Fritz Rumey	July 10, 1918
Oblt. Fritz Otto Bernert	April 23, 1917	*Lt.* Josef Jacobs	July 18, 1918
Lt. Karl-Emil Schaefer	April 26, 1917	*Lt. zur See* Gotthard Sachsenberg	August 5, 1918
Oblt. Kurt Wolff	May 4, 1917	*Hptm.* Franz Walz	August 9, 1918
Lt. Heinrich Gontermann	May 14, 1917	*Lt.* Josef Veltjens	August 16, 1918
Lt. Lothar *Freiherr* von Richthofen	May 14, 1917	*Lt.* Karl Bolle	August 28, 1918
Lt. Carl Allmenröder	June 14, 1917	*Lt.* Theo Osterkamp	September 2, 1918
Hptm. Ernst Brandenburg	June 14, 1917	*Oblt.* Fritz *Ritter* von Röth	September 8, 1918
Hptm. Paul *Freiherr* von Pechmann	July 31, 1917	*Lt.* Otto Könnecke	September 26, 1918
Hptm. Adolf *Ritter* von Tutschek	August 3, 1917	*Lt.* Walter Blume	September 30, 1918
Oblt. Eduard *Ritter* von Dostler	August 6, 1917	*Lt.* Wilhelm Griebsch	September 30, 1918
Fkpt. Peter Strasser	August 30, 1917	*Hptm.* Leo Leonhardy	October 2, 1918
Lt. Max *Ritter* von Müller	September 3, 1917	*Oblt.* Robert *Ritter* von Greim	October 8, 1918
Hptm. Rudolf Kleine	October 4, 1917	*Oblt.* Jürgen von Grone	October 13, 1918
Lt. Walter von Bülow-Bothkamp	October 8, 1917	*Oblt.* Erich Homburg	October 13, 1918
Lt. Curt Wüsthoff	November 22, 1917	*Oblt.* Albert Müller-Kahle	October 13, 1918
Lt. Erwin Böhme	November 24, 1917	*Oblt.* Oskar *Freiherr* von Boenigk	October 25, 1918
Lt. Julius Buckler	December 4, 1917	*Lt.* Franz Büchner	October 25, 1918
Lt. Hans Klein	December 4, 1917	*Lt.* Arthur Laumann	October 25, 1918
Hptm. Eduard *Ritter* von Schleich	December 4, 1917	*Lt.* Oliver *Freiherr* von Beaulieu-Marconnay	October 26, 1918
Hptm. Alfred Keller	December 4, 1917		
Kptlt. Friedrich Christiansen	December 11, 1917	*Lt.* Karl Thom	November 1, 1918
Lt. Heinrich Bongartz	December 23, 1917	*Lt.* Paul Bäumer	November 2, 1918
Oblt. Hermann Fricke	December 23, 1917	*Lt.* Ulrich Neckel	November 8, 1918
Oblt. Hans-Jürgen Horn	December 23, 1917	*Lt.* Carl Degelow	November 9, 1918

Pour le Mérite Winners Alphabetically

Recipient	Date of Award	Recipient	Date of Award
Lt. Carl Allmenröder	June 14, 1917	*Hptm.* Rudolf Kleine	October 4, 1917
Oblt. Ernst *Freiherr* von Althaus	July 21, 1916	*Hptm.* Hermann Köhl	May 21, 1918
Lt. Paul Bäumer	November 2, 1918	*Lt.* Otto Könnecke	September 26, 1918
Lt. Oliver *Freiherr* von Beaulieu-Marconnay	October 26, 1918	*Lt.* Heinrich Kroll	March 29, 1918
		Lt. Arthur Laumann	October 25, 1918
Oblt. Fritz Otto Bernert	April 23, 1917	*Lt.* Gustav Leffers	November 5, 1916
Oblt. Hans Berr	December 4, 1916	*Hptm.* Leo Leonhardy	October 2, 1918
Hptm. Rudolf Berthold	October 12, 1916	*Oberst* Hermann von der Lieth-Thomsen	April 8, 1917
Lt. Walter Blume	September 30, 1918	*Hptm.* Bruno Loerzer	February 12, 1918
Lt. Erwin Böhme	November 24, 1917	*Oblt.* Erich Löwenhardt	May 31, 1918
Hptm. Oswald Boelcke	January 12, 1916	*Lt.* Carl Menckhoff	April 23, 1918
Oblt. Oskar *Freiherr* von Boenigk	October 25, 1918	*Lt.* Max *Ritter* von Müller	September 3, 1917
Lt. Karl Bolle	August 28, 1918	*Oblt.* Albert Müller-Kahle	October 13, 1918
Lt. Heinrich Bongartz	December 23, 1917	*Lt.* Max *Ritter* von Mulzer	July 8, 1916
Hptm. Ernst Brandenburg	June 14, 1917	*Lt.* Ulrich Neckel	November 8, 1918
Lt. Julius Buckler	December 4, 1917	*Lt.* Friedrich Nielebock	June 2, 1918
Oblt. Hans-Joachim Buddecke	April 14, 1916	*Lt.* Theo Osterkamp	September 2, 1918
Lt. Franz Büchner	October 25, 1918	*Lt.* Otto Parschau	July 10, 1916
Lt. Walter von Bülow-Bothkamp	October 8, 1917	*Hptm.* Paul *Freiherr* von Pechmann	July 31, 1917
Kptlt. Horst *Freiherr* Treusch von Buttlar-Brandenfels	April 9, 1918	*Lt.* Fritz Pütter	May 31, 1918
		Lt. Lothar *Freiherr* von Richthofen	May 14, 1917
Kptlt. Friedrich Christiansen	December 11, 1917	*Rittm.* Manfred *Freiherr* von Richthofen	January 12, 1917
Lt. Carl Degelow	November 9, 1918		
Lt. Albert Dossenbach	November 11, 1916	*Lt.* Peter Rieper	July 7, 1918
Oblt. Eduard *Ritter* von Dostler	August 6, 1917	*Oblt.* Fritz *Ritter* von Röth	September 8, 1918
Lt. Wilhelm Frankl	August 12, 1916	*Lt.* Fritz Rumey	July 10, 1918
Oblt. Hermann Fricke	December 23, 1917	*Lt. zur See* Gotthard Sachsenberg	August 5, 1918
Oblt. Hermann Göring	June 2, 1918	*Lt.* Karl-Emil Schaefer	April 26, 1917
Lt. Heinrich Gontermann	May 14, 1917	*Hptm.* Eduard *Ritter* von Schleich	December 4, 1917
Oblt. Robert *Ritter* von Greim	October 8, 1918	*Lt.* Wilhelm Paul Schreiber	June 8, 1918
Lt. Wilhelm Griebsch	September 30, 1918	*Fkpt.* Peter Strasser	August 30, 1917
Oblt. Jürgen von Grone	October 13, 1918	*Lt.* Karl Thom	November 1, 1918
Lt. Walter Höhndorf	July 20, 1916	*Lt.* Emil Thuy	June 30, 1918
Genlt. Ernst von Hoeppner	April 8, 1917	*Hptm.* Adolf *Ritter* von Tutschek	August 3, 1917
Oblt. Erich Homburg	October 13, 1918	*Oblt.* Ernst Udet	April 9, 1918
Oblt. Hans-Jürgen Horn	December 23, 1917	*Lt.* Josef Veltjens	August 16, 1918
Oblt. Max Immelmann	January 12, 1916	*Lt.* Werner Voss	April 8, 1917
Lt. Josef Jacobs	July 18, 1918	*Hptm.* Franz Walz	August 9, 1918
Hptm. Alfred Keller	December 4, 1917	*Lt.* Rudolf Windisch	June 6, 1918
Lt. Hans Kirschstein	June 24, 1918	*Lt.* Kurt Wintgens	July 1, 1916
Oblt. Otto Kissenberth	June 30, 1918	*Oblt.* Kurt Wolff	May 4, 1917
Lt. Hans Klein	December 4, 1917	*Lt.* Curt Wüsthoff	November 22, 1917

Index

Aviation Units:

Bibliography & Glossary

Bibliography
Books

Avci, Cenk. *The Skies of Gallipoli* (Istanbul: Nart Yayincilik, 2003)

Bronnenkant, Lance. *The Imperial German Eagles in World War I: Their Pictures and Postcards*, Volume 1 (Atglen: Schiffer Publishing, 2006)

Bronnenkant, Lance. *The Imperial German Eagles in World War I: Their Pictures and Postcards*, Volume 3 (Atglen: Schiffer Publishing, 2011)

Buddecke, Hans Joachim. *El Schahin (Der Jagdfalke)* (Berlin: Verlag August Scherl, 1918)

Franks, Norman. *Sharks Among Minnows* (London: Grub Street, 2001)

Franks, Norman, Frank Bailey & Rick Duiven. *Casualties of the German Air Service 1914–1920* (London: Grub Street, 1999)

Franks, Norman, Frank Bailey & Russell Guest. *Above The Lines* (London: Grub Street, 1996)

Gengler, Ludwig. *Kampfflieger Rudolf Berthold* (Berlin: Schlieffen-Verlag, 1934)

Grosz, Peter. *Fokker E.I/II* (Berkhamsted: Albatros Productions, 2002)

Grosz, Peter. *Fokker E.IV* (Berkhamsted: Albatros Publications, 1996)

Grosz, Peter. *Halberstadt Fighters* (Berkhamsted: Albatros Publications, 1996)

Hart, Peter. *Somme Success* (Barnsley: Pen & Sword Books, 2001)

Heinemann, Wolfgang. [see *Die Braunschweiger im Weltkriege* below]

Henshaw, Trevor. *The Sky Their Battlefield* (London: Grub Street, 1995)

Immelmann, Franz. Immelmann, *"der Adler von Lille"* (Leipzig: Verlag K.F Koehler, 1942)

Immelmann, Franz (trans. by Claud Sykes). Immelmann, *"The Eagle of Lille"* (London: John Hamilton, unknown)

Immelmann, Max. *Meine Kampfflüge* (Berlin: Verlag August Scherl, 1917)

Kastner, Reinhard. [see *Das Propellerblatt* below]

Möller, Hanns. *Geschichte der Ritter des Ordens "Pour le Mérite" im Weltkrieg – Band 1* (Berlin: Verlag Bernard & Graefe, 1935)

Nowarra, Heinz. *50 Jahre Deutsche Luftwaffe – Band I* (Berlin: Burrath & Schmidt, 1961)

O'Connor, Neal. *Aviation Awards of Imperial Germany in World War I and the Men Who Earned Them*, Volume 4. (Princeton: Foundation for WWI Aviation, 1995)

O'Connor, Neal. *Aviation Awards of Imperial Germany in World War I and the Men Who Earned Them*, Volume 6. (Stratford: Flying Machines Press, 1999)

O'Connor, Neal. *Aviation Awards of Imperial Germany in World War I and the Men Who Earned Them*, Volume 7. (Atglen: Schiffer Publishing, 2002)

Robertson, Bruce. *Air Aces of the 1914–1918 War* (Fallbrook: Aero Publishers, 1959)

Schobachter, Elizabeth. *"Unser Allgäuer Fliegerheld"*; in *Der Stadt Memmingen*, 9 June 1917, pp.1–12.

Sieverts, Dr. Ernst. *"Ein Tag bei meiner alten Feldfliegerabteilung im Westen"*; in O. Daenbruch, *Unsere Luftwaffe im Weltkrieg (II. Folge)* (Leipzig: Kunstverlag 'Bild und Karte', 1917), pp.10–21

The Royal Air Force Museum and Cross & Cockade International. *FE2b/d and Variants in RFC, RAF, RNAS & AFC Service* (London: Cross & Cockade International, 2009)

VanWyngarden, Greg. *Jasta 18, The Red Noses* (Botley: Osprey, 2011)

Werner, Prof. Johannes, *Boelcke: der Mensch, der Flieger, der Führer der deutschen Jagdfliegerei* (Leipzig: Verlag K.F. Koehler, 1932)

Werner, Prof. Johannes (trans. by Claud Sykes). *Knight of Germany: Oswald Boelcke, German Ace* (Novato: Presidio Press, 1991)

Zuerl, Walter. *Pour-le-mérite Flieger* (Munich: Curt Pechstein Verlag, 1938)

Periodicals & Newspapers

Cross & Cockade International (Leicester: Cross & Cockade International) 1995
  26:3 "Maximilian von Mulzer, The Green Knight" by Stephen Lawson

Cross & Cockade Journal (U.S.) (Whittier: The Society for WWI Aero Historians) 1985
  26:2 "The Forgotten Ace. *Ltn.* Kurt Wintgens and His War Letters" by Jeffrey Sands

Das Propellerblatt (Interessengemeinschaft Luftfahrt) 2001, 2006
  1:2 "*Markierungen (2) Flugzeuge der Armee-Abteilung Gaede 1915*" by Reinhard Kastner
  2:17 "*Leutnant Max Ritter von Mulzer Erster Träger des 'Pour-le-Mérite' der bayerischen Fliegertruppe*" by Reinhard Kastner

Die Braunschweiger im Weltkriege (Braunschweig: Verlag von E. Appelhans & Comp.) 1916
  13 "*Mit Immelmann und Mulzer in der Luftschlacht zusammen*" by Wolfgang Heinemann

Die Luftflotte (Berlin: Deutscher Luftflotten-Verein) 1917

Die Woche (Berlin: Verlag August Scherl) 1916

Flugsport (Frankfurt: Verlag Flugsport) 1916

Illustrierte Geschichte des Weltkrieges (Berlin: Union Deutsche Verlagsgesellschaft) 1916

Illustrierte Kriegs-Zeitung (Berlin: Pass & Garleb) 1916

Kriegs-Chronik der Leipziger Neuesten Nachrichten (Leipzig: Verlag Edgar Herfurth) 1916

Over The Front (League of WWI Aviation Historians) 1996
  11:3 "Over the Wine-Dark Sea, Part 5" by Richard Whistler

The Lowell Sun (Lowell) 1916

Glossary

Adjutant (Adj.)	Warrant Officer
Armee-Flug-Park (AFP)	army aviation supply depot
Artillerie-Flieger-Abteilung (AFA)	artillery cooperation aviation unit
Brigadier (Brig.)	Corporal (artillery or cavalry)
Capitaine (Capt.)	Captain
Caporal (Cpl.)	Corporal
Ehrenbecher	honor goblet (usually awarded to airman after 1st victory)
Eindecker	monoplane
Ettapen-Flugzeug-Park (EFP)	army aviation supply depot
Fähnrich	officer candidate
Fahnenjunker	officer cadet or ensign
Feldflieger-Abteilung (FFA)	field aviation unit
Feldflugchef	Chief of Army Field Aviation
Feldwebel (Fw.)	Sergeant
Flieger-Abteilung (FA)	aviation unit
Flieger-Bataillon	aviation battalion
Flieger-Ersatz-Abteilung (FEA)	aviation replacement unit
Fliegertruppe	Air Service
Fokkerstaffel	unit equipped with *Eindecker* aircraft
Gefreiter (Gefr.)	Private 1st Class (army)
General (Gen.)	General
Generalmajor (GenMaj.)	Major General (U.S. Brigadier General)
Generaloberst	Colonel General (U.S. Four-Star General)
Hauptmann (Hptm.)	Captain
Heeresbericht	army reports
Jagdstaffel (Jasta)	fighter unit

Kampfeinsitzer-Kommando (KEK)	single-seat fighter unit
Kampfgeschwader (KG)	fighting squadron
Kapitänleutnant (Kptlt.)	Captain Lieutenant (U.S. Navy full Lieutenant)
Leutnant (Lt.)	2nd Lieutenant
Lieutenant (Lt.)	1st Lieutenant
Luftstreitkräfte	air force
Major (Maj.)	Major
Maréchal-des-Logis (MdL.)	Sergeant (artillery or cavalry)
Oberleutnant (Oblt.)	1st Lieutenant
Oberleutnant zur See (Oblt.z.See)	Senior Lieutenant (U.S. Navy Lieutenant Junior Grade)
Oberst	Colonel
Oberstleutnant (Oberstlt.)	Lieutenant Colonel
Offizier-Stellvertreter (Offz-Stv.)	Warrant Officer
Sergent (Sgt.)	Sergeant
Sous-Lieutenant (Sous-Lt.)	2nd Lieutenant
Staffelführer	commanding officer of a *Staffel*
Unteroffizier (Uffz.)	Corporal
Vizefeldwebel (Vzfw.)	Vice Sergeant or Vice Sergeant Major
Werknummer	factory works number

Color Profile Captions

1. Fokker E.I 15/15 flown by Buddecke, *FFA* 23
Like most other early Fokker *Eindecker* types, Buddecke's first monoplane displayed a clear-doped finish on all of its fabric-covered surfaces. The fabric used seems to have been fairly coarse linen, varnished to produce a fairly opaque buff or beige appearance, glossy when the varnish was newly applied. The large Iron Cross national insignia were marked in large white fields on the wings and on the rudder, which was white overall except for a small area at the base. Like a number of other early E.I's this machine did not carry any cross markings on the fuselage.

2. Fokker E.II 35/15 flown by Buddecke, *FFA* 23
The overall finish of Buddecke's 100 hp Fokker E.II was largely identical to that of E.I 15/15. The serial number appeared in the usual location beneath the wing, but – as was often the case – much of it was apparently obliterated by exhaust fumes or castor oil stains.

3. Fokker E.III 96/15 flown by Buddecke, Turkish *Flieger-Abteilung* 6
Prior to WWI, Turkish aircraft displayed the Ottoman markings of a white crescent moon and star on a red field; this style of national marking was abandoned in the Great War, possibly to avoid confusion with Allied markings. When German aircraft were shipped to Turkey for use with the Ottoman forces, they still bore the usual Iron Cross insignia. For obvious reasons, Muslim Ottoman commanders did not want "their" machines to display the cross insignia. The solution was to over paint the German Iron Cross insignia with a solid black square, leaving a narrow white outline. Fokker E.III 96/15 displayed these markings on wings and fuselage and on its white rudder. As noted, In his book Buddecke himself made a reference to his Fokker as "...my yellow bird with black threatening eyes on the wingtips," a description that certainly indicates a clear-doped linen finish as seen in this profile. Note the absence of wheel covers.

4. Halberstadt D.V flown by Buddecke, *Jasta* 4
Like a number of other Halberstadt D.V's, this machine was camouflaged on all upper and side surfaces. This probably took the form of sprayed tones of dark olive green and reddish or chestnut brown, with the undersides being finished in pale blue. It is evident from Buddecke's writing ("...*unsere braunen Ratten*," as noted in the photo captions) that the brown shade dominated, and the general impression of these aircraft from any distance was of a brownish machine. In common with at least two other Halberstadt fighters of *Jasta* 4, Buddecke's D.V was distinguished by light-colored vertical bands bordering the nation insignia on the fuselage. The color, or colors, of these markings is not recorded but we have chosen light blue as a plausible interpretation.

5. Pfalz D.IIIa 5983/17 flown by Buddecke, *Jasta* 30

Hans-Joachim Buddecke spent only a brief period in *Jasta* 30 in February 1918, but was photographed with this Pfalz D.IIIa 5983/17. It did not display the now-familiar black-bordered orange diamond marking which would soon become the hallmark of the *Staffel*. Instead, Buddecke's Pfalz featured what is believed to be either a stylized heart or a spade from a playing card as a personal motif, painted around the national cross insignia. It is speculated, but not confirmed, that this emblem was black. The remainder of the machine displayed the famous Pfalz factory overall silver finish.

6. Fokker E.IV 176/16 flown by Mulzer, *Abwehrkommando Nord*

This was yet another "plain plane". It apparently displayed only the usual clear-doped finish resulting in light yellowish beige fabric. The metal nose panels and engine cowling were 'engine turned,' resulting in the distinctive swirled effect on the unpainted metal.

7. Pfalz E.II 226/15 flown by Mulzer, *FFA* 62

Mulzer's Pfalz monoplane bore the typical factory finish. The Pfalz E-types were apparently covered with very white fabric, most likely bleached linen or linen treated with white-pigmented dope. This is confirmed by a well-known color-printed advertisement for the Pfalz firm that appeared in *Motor* magazine, as well as a statement given in an interview by veteran German pilot Kurt Weil: "…the old Aviatiks were snow white, with sometimes black linings or corners… and so, as I remember, were the first Pfalz monoplanes… These aircraft were brilliant white – so white that if you flew in sunlight, they looked transparent from the ground." He also recalled that, due to the black borders on the fuselage and wings, these white machines were often called "flying death announcements." The metal struts, engine cowlings and wheel covers of these Pfalz were painted in a glossy black. National insignia appeared on both surfaces of the wings and elevators, the fuselage sides, and the rudder. The serial numbers were generally marked in very small characters on the fuselage sides behind the fuel tank, the top of the rudder, and the leading edge of each elevator.

8. Fokker E.I 5/15 flown by Wintgens, *FFA* 6b & *FFA* 48

Wintgens' E.5/15 was equipped with a Parabellum LMG 14 and had the high wing mounting of the Fokker M 5KMG. The padded headrest was supposed to help steady the pilot's head while aiming. This machine was shipped from the Fokker factory on 24 June 1915, and the profile depicts it in its initial plain finish. Later on – during early July 1915 – Wintgens was temporarily transferred to *Feldflieger Abteilung* 48 in *Armee Abteilung Gaede*. It was then decorated with the black rudder and black/white fuselage bands which characterized aircraft of that *Armee*.

9. Fokker E.IV 124/15 flown by Wintgens, various units

Wintgen's two-gun E.IV 124/15 was yet another example of an aircraft in unadorned factory finish. Like most other E.IV's, this machine was marked with the national insignia on both sides of the fuselage, and displayed the military serial number beneath the trailing edge of the wing.

10. Halberstadt D.II flown by Wintgens, unit unknown

Wintgens' D.II bore a pale overall finish that was very common on the type. The question among marking enthusiasts has long been: exactly what color was this light finish? It may have simply been the result of clear-doped linen, which would present a very pale yellowish appearance – with the plywood panels on the nose area painted to match. Josef Jacobs described one of the machines he flew at the *Jastaschule* as a "white Halberstadt" (10 January 1917) – whatever that means. The translucency of the wings apparent in many photos would support a clear-doped interpretation; in these photos the black and white national markings on the upper wings are distinctly darker and more opaque than the rest of the wing. Another interpretation is that the Halberstadts were painted a very light blue or blue-gray; many two-seaters of this time featured such finishes as a type of "sky camouflage". A painting of a Halberstadt by British D.H.2 ace Sir Robert Saundby (who certainly saw such machines in combat) seems to support the light blue-gray or gray theory. It is entirely possible that both finishes were in use, and our profile presents one plausible interpretation of the overall light-colored finish.

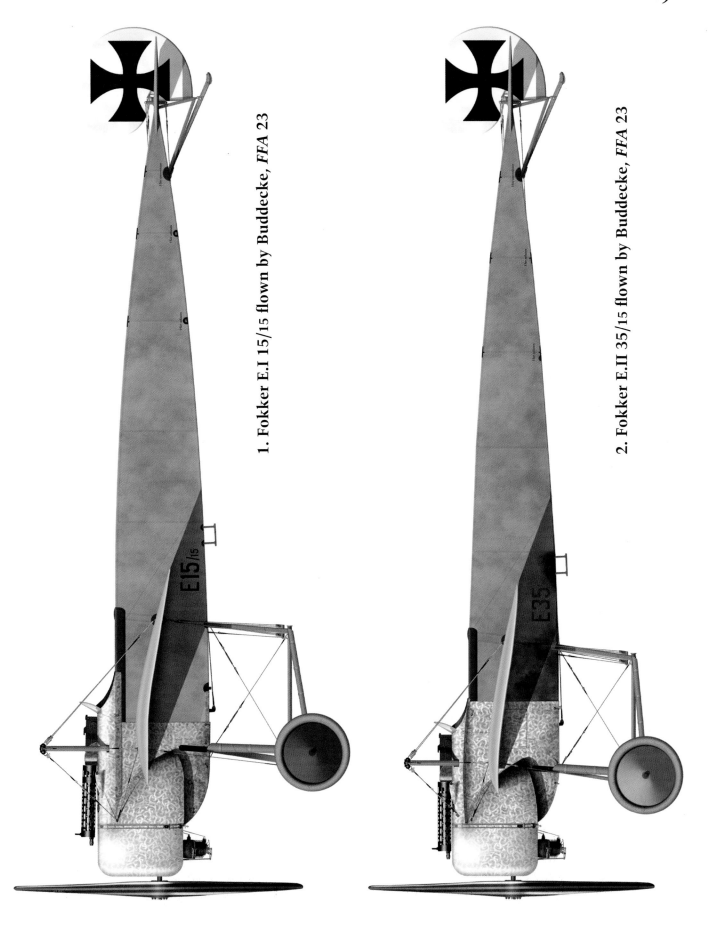

1. Fokker E.I 15/15 flown by Buddecke, *FFA* 23

2. Fokker E.II 35/15 flown by Buddecke, *FFA* 23

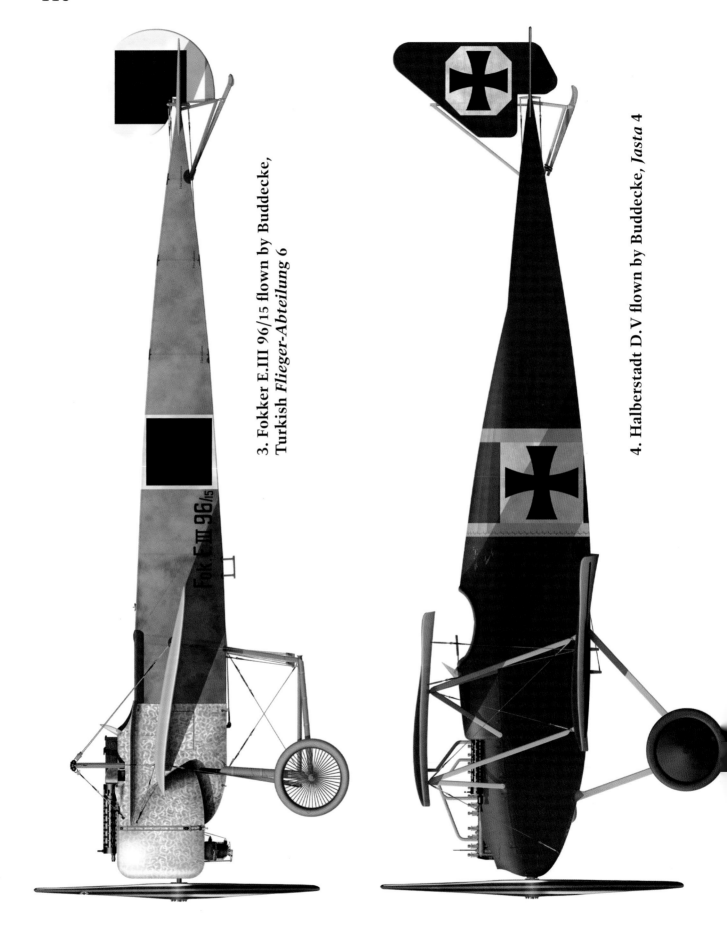

3. Fokker E.III 96/15 flown by Buddecke,
Turkish *Flieger-Abteilung* 6

4. Halberstadt D.V flown by Buddecke, *Jasta* 4

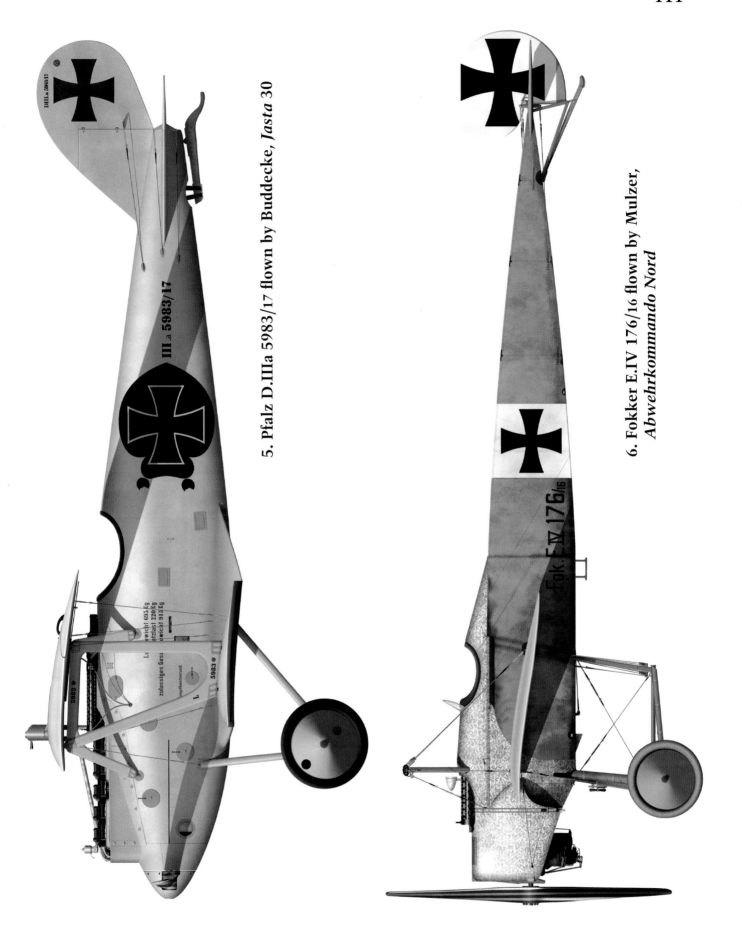

5. Pfalz D.IIIa 5983/17 flown by Buddecke, *Jasta 30*

6. Fokker E.IV 176/16 flown by Mulzer, *Abwehrkommando Nord*

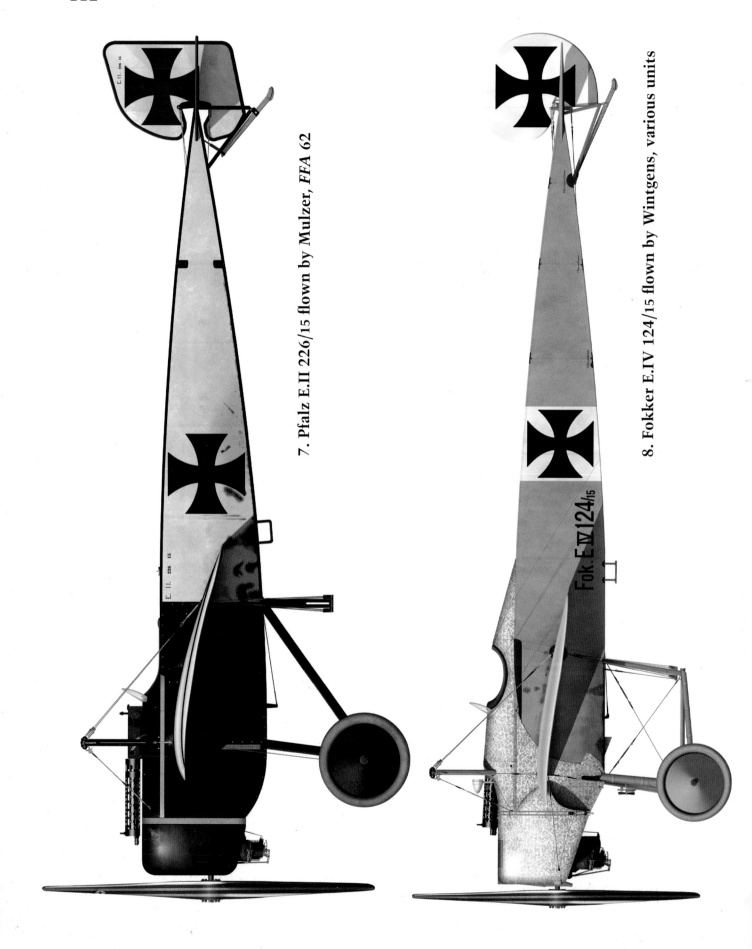

7. Pfalz E.II 226/15 flown by Mulzer, *FFA 62*

8. Fokker E.IV 124/15 flown by Wintgens, *various units*